Presented to:

_____

From:

_____

31-Day BLESSINGS JOURNEY

A Devotional that Will Transform Your Stress into Blessings

by Dana Susan Beasley

Copyright © 2015 by Dana Susan Beasley
Published by AngelArts, A Creative Arts Agency & Publishing House
3107 West Colorado Avenue #303, Colorado Springs, Colorado 80904
Website: www.AngelArts.biz, **Email:** info@angelarts.biz

All rights reserved. No part of this book may be reproduced in any form or by an electronic or mechanical means including information storage and retrieval systems without the written permission of the copyright holder.

Scripture taken from The Message. Copyright © 1993, 1994, 1995, 1996, 2000, 2001, 2002. Used by permission of NavPress Publishing Group.

Scripture taken from the NEW AMERICAN STANDARD BIBLE®, Copyright © 1960,1962,1963,1968,1971,1972,1973,1975,1977,1995 by The Lockman Foundation. Used by permission.

Scripture also taken from THE HOLY BIBLE, NEW INTERNATIONAL VERSION®, NIV® Copyright © 1973, 1978, 1984, 2011 by Biblica, Inc.® Used by permission. All rights reserved worldwide.

First Edition
Cover photo: **Irochka** (Adobe Stock)
Interior artwork: Adobe Stock—Lines and picture frame, **logistock;** Birds and flowers, **one**
Cover design and interior design: Dana Susan Beasley

ISBN-13: 978-0692586075
ISBN-10: 0692586075

Printed in the United States of America.

Dedication

First and foremost, I dedicate this book to **my Lord and Savior Jesus Christ** who brought me through incredible stress and walked with me step by step. I praise Him for the blessings He's brought in my life, chiefly that of getting to know Him a little more each and every day.

I dedicate this book to my husband, Travis, who has walked with me also during exceedingly stressful times, and though he has struggled greatly himself, he kept putting his eyes back on Jesus and constantly reached toward God's greater blessings despite the overwhelming fear at times he felt. That is true courage and integrity!

To Sam, who is the reason why I keep battling day after day, even when it seems like I'm riding on a merry-go-around with no way off, or slogging through mud, sinking faster than I can climb out. You inspire me everyday to do better, to be better, and to never quit.

Acknowledgments

How do I thank everyone who went along with me on this journey? Who stood by me in the darkest of days?

First, there are my parents, Ann and Dale Neal, who thought of a creative and concrete way to help our family. Without them, we would not be experiencing the blessings we are experiencing today. Their support, both emotionally and financially, has made a huge difference in our lives. Thank you for believing in us, even when times were bleakest.

My sister Diana and her husband Tim were also a huge support during times when all seemed to be lost. I will never forget the night my sister and I sat in a cabin on the Baltic Sea, a cruise generously provided by my sister and my parents, and I was weeping because of hearing some dire financial news from home. Upon hearing our need, my sister did not bat an eye and her husband agreed. They lovingly took care of us. The next day I prayed for an opportunity to bless them as they had blessed us, because really, in the end, financial matters are just temporary. I was beyond blessed that I could bless both of them with the circumstances that unfolded over the next few months. That in itself is another story, a true testimony to God's amazing way of orchestrating events.

To my father-in-law Kent Beasley, who helped and supported Travis through his architectural license exams. His concern and love was very much appreciated! We are definitely blessed today because of his investment.

To my sister-in-law Jayne and brother Dan, who generously helped when we were in need. For Jayne who always believed in my endeavors and prayed for me consistently and with much joy. Who could see the maturity and the grace God brought into our lives. Her joy was contagious!

To Jacob, my nephew, who got an inside look at the stress we Beasleys were enduring. He loved us and battled with us during these turbulent times. Without you, dear nephew, I doubt that we would have a family. You saved our lives. Your love kept me going when my life seemed like a black hole.

And all my family members. You all stood by us and prayed and listened. I am truly blessed to be a Neal with this huge family! It would take a book in itself to thank you all and tell you how much I love each and everyone of you.

To Deborah Nelson, who challenged me and gave me the vision of a work at homeschooling lifestyle. It was your words that propelled me to embrace entrepreneurialism and homeschooling. Years of our discussions of working at home brought me to where I am today.

To our friends at the Navigator Metro Friends Bible study, who faithfully prayed for us every step of the way. Your prayers and generosity sustained us and blessed us immeasurably. You gave us tangible reminders of God's love and care.

To our friend Doug Prensner, whom I've known since 1989. Thank you for listening, for guiding me, for showing me the love of the Savior. You walked with me when I felt that I didn't matter to God. You are a demonstration of His love. Thanks also goes to his ***wife Jean*** who prayed and was such a support in these stressful times.

To my college friend Jean VanOrdstrand, who believed in me, encouraged me, and showed me so much loyal friendship all these years.

To Helping Our Members Educate Homeschool support group, who also prayed for us every step of the way. Who brought meals after our dog died. Who helped us in our homeschooling journey.

To Victor Matos and our church, Harvest Downtown. We could not have gotten through this without you and the support of the body. The generosity and love of the church blew us away. Victor, your shepherd's heart blessed me many times over.

To Zoey Lee, who embraced my nephew and loved him like a son. I will never forget how you came over when Rascal died, helped Travis load him into the car, and sat with me as I worked through my grief. You are a true friend! I am sad that you moved away but excited for you on your new journey.

To Tammie Polk, my client, business partner, and friend from Tennessee who grasped the vision of my work and believed in me and challenged me. You are a huge blessing!

To Dahlyn Ribeck, who didn't bat an eye about spoiling us with her love by bringing us dinner. You demonstrated true love in action. All from a Facebook message! I was indeed blessed by your tender loving care and Christ-like act.

To Linda Hamilton, who thought nothing of sending us a DVD of The Hobbit. Our chats over Facebook were encouraging and uplifting. Your generosity blessed our family many times over.

To Raquel Younglove, who blessed me with her dedicated work in helping my son. It was a true blessing to finish this book while sitting in your pleasant office, the gentle sweet little waterfall in the background. It was an oasis in a time of chaos as I forged ahead, looking for answers and seeking breakthrough for my son and for my whole family.

Contents

Introduction
Page 11

How to Use this Devotional
Page 19

Devotionals
Page 23

Devotional Review
Page 231

About the Author
Page 233

About the Publisher
Page 235

Would you Like to Receive More Blessings?
Page 237

Give the Gift of Blessing!
Page 238

"How blessed all those in whom you live whose lives become roads you travel; They wind through lonesome valleys, come upon brooks, discover cool springs and pools brimming with rain! God-traveled, these roads curve up the mountain, and at the last turn—Zion! God in full view!"

—Psalm 84:5–7, *The Message*

Introduction

STRESS. OUR WORLD TODAY SCREAMS IT. Our world demands it of us. The news inundates us with it. You know what I'm talking about because like me, you live it. If you are in the habit of turning on the news, stress endlessly parades itself with each murder, each bombing, each layoff. In social media, it's rampant, like a runaway train.

The pressure put on our kids and put on us parents to be perfect crushes us. It crushes children from a young age. Many schools these days, especially with Common Core, drum the joy of learning out of our kids. Our jobs put pressure on us. Everyone, it seems, wants everything right now—or even better yet, yesterday.

Just living as a citizen puts crushing demands on us. The red tape chokes us and more so every single day. Renewing driver's licenses, getting tags for cars, protecting Social Security numbers, even just the amount of computer passwords one has to keep up with!

These last seven years have brought incredible economic stress. Millions have left the job force. More businesses are closed each year than are opened. Many have lost health care insurance. Terrorism is a clear and present danger and circles ever closer to us in America.

Fear and stress is the mantra that is expressed day and night, night and day. It paralyzes, it stymies, and it kills.

Blessings Journey

Yes, it kills. Stress leads to heart attacks. Stress causes cancer. Cancer kills us. Then there's Post Traumatic Stress Disorder... It's really not a nice version of the *If You Give a Mouse a Cookie* book!

So what can be done about it? Can anything be done about it? Is stress just a *fate di compli* that we need to resign our lives to? Is there an antidote?

Absolutely yes, there is an antidote! And it's found in the Bible. The Bible is rich with this antidote. I'm not saying it's easy, but it's a journey worth taking.

Because the process of this journey creates growth and maturity, and that produces fruit. This new life that you experience through this journey transforms stress into incredible blessings.

How do I know this? Because I am living it, I have lived it, I will live it again. Every human being must face adversity. The question is, what will we do with this adversity?

My Journey of Stress

LET ME BEGIN BY DESCRIBING MY JOURNEY a little bit and how I came to write about transforming stress into blessings. Where do I even say where the journey began? Stress, like everyone else, has always been in my life to one degree or another. After all, in 1998 I was diagnosed with Cumulative Stress Disorder, which thankfully I was healed from after much prayer and alternative therapy.

But I suppose this story really began on 9/11. September 11, 2001, when I witnessed on television the horrific tumbling of the Twin Towers, sitting in my 1898 parlor holding my nine-month old son, I realized that I had buried myself. My husband and I had newly moved to this quaint painted-lady house that needed remodeling.

Introduction

Restoring old houses had always been our dream, but as I watched the terrifying news, the reality of what we had done started to crumble around me.

Another Realization

THEN AS OUR SON, Sam, grew into a toddler, another realization came. He was not the child I expected. Something was different about him. He walked on his toes. He didn't play with other children. He was sometimes aggressive and had disproportional meltdowns when he got hurt. And then there were really tough developmental challenges that left us feeling defeated, worn out, and baffled. My husband and I thought it was behavior. I felt desperate, alone, and forsaken. I bottled it inside and "soldiered on."

When our child grew into school-age, we chose to send him to a Christian private school. We thought this was the perfect answer. All our problems would be solved. But then more reality started piling on. The demands of the school stressed our son so much that in first grade our chiropractor found his colon was impacted and blocked.

A child, six years of age, in so much stress that his gut is impacted!

Every day, Travis would take Sam to school and we had our "fish bowl" experience as he would have a meltdown walking to the car which was parked on the street. Every day, I would pick up Sam from school and we would hear a bad report. Every single day.

As part of our tuition discount for going to the school as members of the church, we were required to attend church every Sunday. Now don't misunderstand, we are regular church-goers and we delight in going to church. But the pressure of the **requirement** of going to church to check it off someone else's list took the joy out of going to church. It became another have-to. We began to realize it wasn't a good fit, especially since Sam had a very hard time sitting through the services.

We met with the minister and told him what was going on. And that's when my husband said the words: "We are blessed, *not* stressed."

My husband's words made me think. I liked the catchiness of what he said. I liked the visual and entrepreneurial possibilities. Later I turned his saying into a bumper sticker, then tshirts, mugs, and other paraphernalia.

But that perspective stuck in my mind and it stuck in his mind. We started to pray, *"God, where do you want us?"* This led us on a journey, one that we're still on today. First we asked, *"Where do you want us to go to church?"* That led us to change after change until we found the church that **really** treats us like one of the family. Then we asked, *"Where do you want us to live?"* So we bought another house that could serve us better with the crucial needs we had with Sam. We found a bigger property with three bathrooms, a garage, and land surrounding it. We didn't feel like we were in a fish bowl anymore. We remodeled the old house and turned it into a vacation rental. Then, two months after we had moved into the new house, we asked again, *"Where do you want Sam to go to school?"*

The Last Straw

THE ANSWER—AFTER FINDING OUT THAT OUR SON had been forced to take an achievement test in **first grade** and not done well and the teacher acted as if it was the end of the world—we found was to homeschool him.

Introduction

That decision opened up our world but certainly brought on new stresses. However, I was determined not to make school stressful, so I designed it completely different from the traditional classroom. We finished remodeling our old house the very last day of Sam's first grade in the private school and Travis literally scooped him out of the classroom, talked to no one on the way out, and brought him home. We never looked back. We didn't even bother to find out if he passed first grade or not and what grades he had received. Because of this decision, I was eventually able to finally see that my son is high-functioning Autistic, he had dysgraphia, and suffered with sensory processing issues. My husband had similar challenges and now we recognize they both most likely have Aspergers Syndrome.

An Empty House

THAT FIRST SUMMER WENT WELL with the new vacation rental business. But that was 2008. I think you know what happened next. After that summer, the house sat empty. We had to pay two mortgages. At the same time, my husband's job was cut back. His paychecks were delayed. The stress all around us was deafening. Foreclosure loomed on the horizon, and I kept wondering, *"Why God? We did what you wanted us to do!"* Bitterness started to overcome me. But I chose to stop it in its tracks.

And the only way I knew how to transform stress is by reading and applying the Bible.

As a college student, my life had been transformed forever by studying the Bible. That first semester at Colorado State University, I was a rebel into all the wrong things. I ran away from God, involved in the partying lifestyle because I felt accepted there. But God pursued me and through new friends brought The Navigators into my life. My mentors taught me how to study the Bible. I

found I loved it. Studying the Bible completely changed me and is still changing me to this day. The Bible became foundational to me.

So there I was facing the greatest stress of my life, financial disaster all around me. As He has done many times, God spoke to me in a profound dream. I was on top of a mountain, and God/Jesus was holding my left hand, and to the left of Him were friends lined up in a row. Many friends. We all bumped down that mountainside, and we would come to hurdle after hurdle where we would have to fly over it to get to the other side, further down the mountain. Each time I approached the hurdle, I would be afraid. But God would squeeze my hand and we would fly over that bump and it was fun! Kind of like a roller coaster. Then we finally got to the bottom and I plunged into a pool, like one of those water slides at a water park. I plunged so fast in that pool that I was drowning. Panic went through me. I reached up my hand. Jesus caught it, and I stood on the side of that pool, laughing. So much joy filled me that it was more joy than I have ever felt before. I had truly accomplished something big. And God was with me the whole time.

My Heartbeat

AFTER THAT DREAM, WHENEVER STRESSES WOULD COME, I would remember, and I would imagine God squeezing my hand. I went through hurdle after hurdle. I don't know if I am still in the pool overwhelmed by life's circumstances, awaiting His rescue, or if I have been rescued already. It doesn't matter. Because I know that He who promised me that I would get through this with joy and laughter is faithful. He doesn't lie. He loves me and I matter to Him and He values me. This is my heartbeat now.

But I could not have come to this transformation without reading the Scriptures. In the midst of those days before the foreclosure of our rental property, I was deter-

Introduction

mined to not let stress beat me. I was determined to allow God to transform that stress into blessings. And I wanted my time in the Word to be a blessing to others who had been through that same process. Because my mission in life is this:

> "Blessed be the God and Father of our Lord Jesus Christ, the Father of mercies and God of all comfort, who comforts us in all our affliction so that we will be able to comfort those who are in any affliction with the comfort with which we ourselves are comforted by God."
> —2 Corinthians 1:3–4, *New American Standard Bible*

I decided to study the antidote of stress. And that is blessings. So I spent nearly two years studying this topic in the Bible and journaling about it. We discussed it in our homeschooling. I applied the lessons learned. It changed my life and the life of my family.

After my studying, I created a 30-day online devotional that many people have been blessed by. But I want this message to impact more people so I am stepping up my game and printing it in book form.

Because I want to offer this comfort to you. Your stress *can be transformed into blessings!*

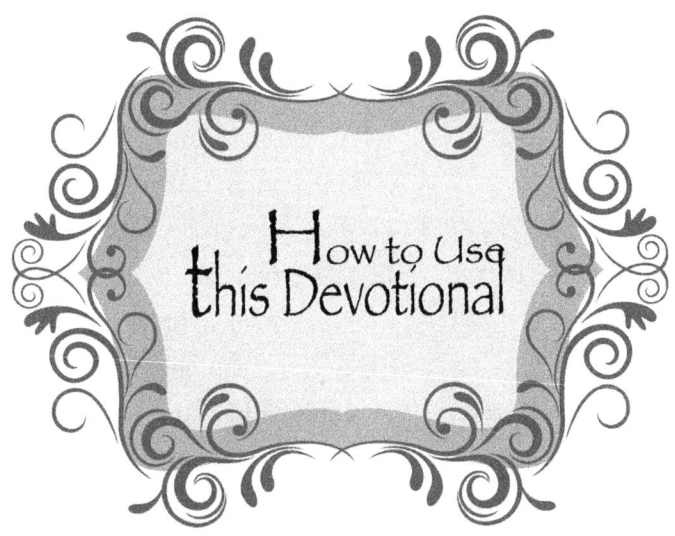

How to Use this Devotional

BLESSINGS. YOU ARE IN FOR A HEAP OF IT IN THIS DEVOTIONAL BOOK!

I am so excited to have you along on this Blessings Journey!

For over two years, I studied this topic in my personal devotions and shared the lessons learned as part of our homeschooling.

As I described in the chapter before, at times I thought I would drown in stress. But God has been faithful to me, holding my hand through every difficult and dark step. And through it all I have discovered tremendous blessings and closeness to my Lord and Savior.

What to Expect

WHETHER YOU WANT TO USE THIS for your personal time with the Lord, as family devotions, or in your homeschool, as you dig in deep you will become closer to Jesus, learn to let go of your stress, and discover new ways to be a vehicle for God's glory.

Each day's devotional is structured to give you time to worship our Lord, to be inspired to go deeper in prayer, learn about blessings from a biblical perspective, and apply these lessons to your life.

Blessings Journey

As you read and apply the Scriptures, your stress will be transformed into blessings! You may want to write in the space provided or the blank spaces after the Scripture so you can use it as a devotional prayer journal. I have lovingly designed this book so it could be your own blessings journal!

Start with a prayer for the Holy Spirit to open the eyes of your heart to the Father, to recognize the presence of Jesus. Then sing the song that I have suggested for worship or sing your favorite song. YouTube or GodTube are great resources for this. I have spent much time in finding praise songs that will encourage you, lift you up, and lead you into the lesson time, but you sing the songs that most fill you with worship and prepare your heart.

Then read the Scripture. I have provided both the broader context of the Scripture and the key verses having to do with the topic of Blessing. Read the entire passage in whatever translation you prefer. After you read it and meditate on what it says, if you want to, free-write or discuss in your family the answer to the two questions, *"What does God say about blessings?"* and *"What is my response?"*

Holy Spirit Guidance

THE MORE YOU PERSONALIZE SCRIPTURE, letting it seep into your heart and letting the Holy Spirit guide you, the more you will be blessed and the less stress you will have. Or better yet, God will give you the strength to face your stress and as a result you will wrangle that stress into blessings! (Of course, you have to be careful not to take passages out of context and add or subtract from what is being said in the text you are looking at, as well as to take the whole Bible into consideration.)

Then read the devotional thoughts I have provided either to yourself or to your family if you are using this as a group devotional. I have also included helpful re-

How to Use this Devotional

sources that will give you a deeper knowledge of the topic of blessings as well as a thoughtful challenge to help you further apply the message.

Also included is a suggested activity if you would like to use this as part of your homeschool or family devotional. After the reading and/or activity, spend time in focused prayer to find ways to apply the lesson you have learned.

Many blessings as you journey with me through this book. I will leave you with one of my favorite blessings:

"The LORD bless you,
and keep you;
The LORD make His face
shine on you,
And be gracious to
you;
The LORD lift up His
countenance on
you,
And give you peace."
—Numbers 6:25–26,
New American Standard Bible

Prayer

Dear Lord Jesus, help us to see Your tremendous blessings, to open our eyes, recognize Your presence here with us, and teach us your heart so that our hearts will be transformed and grow closer to You. *In Jesus' Name, Amen.*

Worship

"Open the Eyes of My Heart"
Phillips, Craig & Dean

Scripture

Genesis 1

Blessings Journey

Genesis 1:20–31, *NASB*

Then God said, "Let the waters teem with swarms of living creatures, and let birds fly above the earth in the open expanse of the heavens." God created the great sea monsters and every living creature that moves, with which the waters swarmed after their kind, and every winged bird after its kind; and God saw that it was good. God blessed them, saying, "Be fruitful and multiply, and fill the waters in the seas, and let birds multiply on the earth." There was evening and there was morning, a fifth day.

Then God said, "Let the earth bring forth living creatures after their kind: cattle and creeping things and beasts of the earth after their kind"; and it was so. God made the beasts of the earth after their kind, and the cattle after their kind, and everything that creeps on the ground after its kind; and God saw that it was good.

Then God said, "Let Us make man in Our image, according to Our likeness; and let them rule over the fish of the sea and over the birds of the sky and over the cattle and over all the earth, and over every creeping thing that creeps on the earth." God created man in His own image, in the image of God He created him; male and female He created them. God blessed them; and God said to them, "Be fruitful and multiply, and fill the earth, and subdue it; and rule over the fish of the sea and over the birds of the sky and over every living thing that moves on the earth." Then God said, "Behold, I have given you every plant yielding seed that is on the surface of all the earth, and every tree which has fruit yielding seed; it shall be food for you; and to every beast of the earth and to every bird of the sky and to every thing that moves on the earth which has life, I have given every green plant for food"; and it was so. God saw all that He had made, and behold, it was very good. And there was evening and there was morning, the sixth day.

 # Day 1

What Does God Say About Blessings?

_____
_____
_____
_____
_____
_____
_____
_____
_____
_____

What Is My Response?

_____
_____
_____
_____
_____
_____
_____
_____
_____
_____

For Further Study

Hebrew Meaning of Bless
http://www.ancient-hebrew.org/27_bless.html

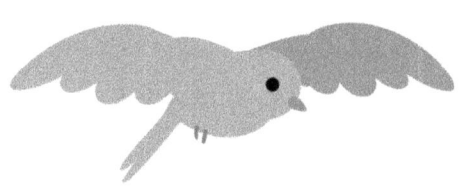

Devotional Thoughts

ABUNDANCE AND BLESSING, you can't separate them. To be blessed is to be granted and commanded to do our part to be fruitful and increase in number. God blessed both creatures (all kinds of animals) and humans, then tied it directly into abundance, fruitfulness, productivity. The earth was to be a blessing, too, a resource for food. To subdue the earth to rule over every living creature. We were given the role of Kings and Queens, as sons and daughters of the King of Kings.

And God's creation was very good. Very whole and complete. To be blessed is to be whole, abundant, productive, and provided for. The dictionary definition of "bless" is to invoke divine favor upon a person. It is a rite of consecration, to give someone a cherished thing or attribute, to thank or express gratitude, to use it as an expression of surprise, endearment, or gratitude.

Our English word bless comes from the "Old English *blēdsian, blētsian,* based on *blōd* **'blood'** (i.e., originally perhaps *'**mark or consecrate with blood**'*). The meaning was influenced by its being used to translate Latin **benedicere *'to praise, worship,'*** and later by association with **bliss**."

That definition comes from my Apple dictionary app. To me, it is very interesting that the origin of bless has the connotation of blood in it. And its ties to the word

# Day 1

bliss. Ultimate blessing is based on the finished work of Jesus Christ, who died on the cross so that none would perish, but have eternal life. That is indeed ultimate bliss, ultimate blessing!

Response

AS I READ THIS PASSAGE, I was encouraged to keep doing what God has called me to do and then to trust Him for the results—abundance and productivity.

I am living out this application right now as I use the talents and gifts God has given me to live out my calling as a publisher, teacher, and encourager. I don't know what the results will be, but I am trusting God for abundance and productivity and my deepest desire—that you will be tremendously blessed by my work!

Encouragement/ Challenge

SO WHAT ARE YOUR CALLINGS? Are you living them? Are you doing everything God has empowered you to do then trusting Him with the results?

Activity

GO FOR A WALK IN NATURE, in your own backyard or in a park, a zoo, or nature preserve. Take along a sketchbook and as you observe

Blessings Journey

one of God's creations, draw it and write, *"What purpose does this creation have in God's design?"*

Prayer

Dear Heavenly Father, thank You so much for the beautiful world You have created. Thank You for creating us in Your image. Help us to be faithful in the callings You have given us. We leave the results up to You. You are a God of abundance and we praise You! *In Jesus' Name, Amen.*

"The LORD bless you,
and keep you;
The LORD make His face
shine on you,
And be gracious to you;
The LORD lift up His
countenance on you,
And give you peace."
—Numbers 6:25–26, *New American Standard Bible*

Blessings Journey Day 2

Prayer

Dear Lord Jesus, we depend on You for everything we have and are. Help us to be real with You, to give our hearts and minds completely to You. Thank You for being there for us always. *In Jesus' Name, Amen.*

Worship

"All I Need Is You"
Hillsong United

Scripture

Luke 6

Luke 6:17–26, *NASB*

Jesus came down with them and stood on a level place; and there was a large crowd of His disciples, and a great throng of people from all Judea and Jerusalem and the coastal region of Tyre and Sidon, who had come to hear Him and to be healed of their diseases; and those who were troubled with unclean spirits were being cured. And all the people were trying to touch Him, for power was coming from Him and healing them all.

The Beatitudes

And turning His gaze toward His disciples, He began to say, "Blessed are you who are poor, for yours is the kingdom of God. Blessed are you who hunger now, for you shall be satisfied. Blessed are you who weep now, for you shall laugh. Blessed are you when men hate you, and ostracize you, and insult you, and scorn your name as evil, for the sake of the Son of Man. Be glad in that day and leap for joy, for behold, your reward is great in heaven. For in the same way their fathers used to treat the prophets. But woe to you who are rich, for you are receiving your comfort in full. Woe to you who are well-fed now, for you shall be hungry. Woe to you who laugh now, for you shall mourn and weep. Woe to you when all men speak well of you, for their fathers used to treat the false prophets in the same way."

 # Day 2

What Does God Say About Blessings?

_____
_____
_____
_____
_____
_____
_____
_____
_____
_____

What Is My Response?

_____
_____
_____
_____
_____
_____
_____
_____
_____

For Further Study

Historical Information on Sermon on the Mount
(The passage in Luke is called the Sermon on the Plain)
https://en.wikipedia.org/wiki/Sermon_on_the_Mount

Devotional Thoughts

WHAT AM I TRUSTING IN? Who do I look to for strength? Is it my "riches" or do I trust in God? In Matthew, it says "blessed are the poor in spirit." Well, I'm certainly not "rich" and I have a lot of needs, both for myself and my family. We are beginning to recognize the needs, and openly acknowledge them. We don't pretend we "have it all together." We don't. Not financially, mentally, physically, organizationally, relationally... We need God and we know it.

I think that's where blessing comes from—recognizing our need for God and thirsting for the kingdom of God, both as "heaven on earth" and one day when all will be healed, our bodies restored, and we never lack for anything.

Response

I ACKNOWLEDGE TO GOD AND TO YOU that I need His help in all I'm doing—in my parenting, my marriage, my homeschooling, my business, my finances, my son's needs, and yes, especially this book. I could not have done it without God's inspiration! In fact, I am nothing and nobody without Jesus. It's only by utter dependence on Him that I am able to bring you these words of encouragement.

Day 2

Encouragement/Challenge

In what ways are you depending on your own strength rather than on God's? Spend some time acknowledging your weaknesses/challenges to Jesus. Give them to Him with open hands and heart. Depend on Him with all your strength of being.

Activity

Have your children draw a map of Galilee using your Bible or online reference site such as Wikipedia. Locate the city of Capernaum. Go on Google Maps and see it from a satellite view. Imagine yourselves standing there on the plain or the hill listening to Jesus' sermon. How would you feel? What would you be thinking? How would you be forever changed?

Prayer

Dear Lord Jesus, we praise You that you are able to handle all our challenges, that we can utterly depend on You. Right now we give you our weaknesses and our shortcomings. We thank You in advance that You will use those shortcomings for tremendous blessing, both for ourselves and those around us. *In Jesus' Name, Amen.*

Blessings Journey

"The LORD bless you,
and keep you;
The LORD make His face
shine on you,
And be gracious to you;
The LORD lift up His
countenance on you,
And give you peace."

—Numbers 6:25–26, *New American Standard Bible*

Prayer

God of all blessing, we thank You for giving to us so abundantly that You sent Your Son to die for us. You held nothing back. Help us to hold nothing back as we come to You and Your Word. *In Jesus' Name, Amen.*

Worship

"Heart of Worship"
https://www.youtube.com/watch?v=nkvMt-KKVKA

Scripture

Proverbs 10:22, *NASB*

It is the blessing of the Lord that makes rich, And He adds no sorrow to it.

What Does God Say About Blessings?

_____
_____
_____
_____
_____
_____
_____
_____
_____

What Is My Response?

_____
_____
_____
_____
_____
_____
_____
_____
_____

Day 3

For Further Study

More Information About the Origins of the Word Blessed
http://www.answers.com/Q/What_is_the_Greek_word_for_'blessed'

Devotional Thoughts

WHERE DOES PROSPERITY COME FROM? What is wealth? Being truly rich comes from the Lord and there is no guilt in it. It is the Lord that will put us back together again—we look forward to His rich abundance—supplying every need—and the joy that will come out of it.

Response

I NEED TO KEEP DOING WHAT GOD has called me to do and trust in Him for the results. Sometimes the lesson and the response is just a matter of perseverance, of a word I'm not too fond of sometimes—waiting!

Encouragement/Challenge

Who are you counting on to make yourself "rich," whether financially, relationally, etc. Who are you trusting in for your abundance? Do you really believe that God will supply your every need? What are the blessings or riches that He has already given you?

Activity

Make a blessing tree. On a big poster board, draw the basic outline of a tree trunk and branches. Have your family draw and cut out leaves to go on that tree. On the leaves, write the blessings that God has given you individually and as a family. Hang it up in your living room for all to see! This is a great activity for Thanksgiving!

Prayer

Heavenly Father, thank You that true wealth and abundance comes from You. Thank You that You are our Source. And through You, we can have joy no matter what the circumstances. Help us to keep persevering in the challenges we face, knowing and trusting that You will supply all our needs. *In Jesus' Name, Amen.*

 Day 3

"The LORD bless you,
and keep you;
The LORD make His face
shine on you,
And be gracious to you;
The LORD lift up His
countenance on you,
And give you peace."

—Numbers 6:25–26, *New American Standard Bible*

Blessings Journey Day 4

Prayer

Oh Lamb of God, we truly adore You heart, soul, mind, and body. We thank You for sacrificing everything so we could be close to You, our Savior. We love You and praise You. *In Jesus' Name, Amen.*

Worship

"Revelation Song"
Kari Jobe

Scripture

Revelations 5

Revelations 5:11-14, *NASB*

Then I looked, and I heard the voice of many angels around the throne and the living creatures and the elders; and the number of them was myriads of myriads, and thousands of thousands, saying with a loud voice, "Worthy is the Lamb that was slain to receive power and riches and wisdom and might and honor and glory and blessing."

And every created thing which is in heaven and on the earth and under the earth and on the sea, and all things in them, I heard saying, "To Him who sits on the throne, and to the Lamb, be blessing and honor and glory and dominion forever and ever."

And the four living creatures kept saying, "Amen" And the elders fell down and worshiped.

 Day 4

What Does God Say About Blessings?

_____
_____
_____
_____
_____
_____
_____
_____
_____

What Is My Response?

_____
_____
_____
_____
_____
_____
_____
_____
_____

For Further Study

A Deeper Look at the Revelation Song
https://www.youtube.com/watch?v=HDjHOJw5bM
Keywords: Revelation Song, Mercy Seat, Easter, The Passion

The above link tends to be moved a lot, so search for the keywords and you will find it.

This video has some graphic images of Jesus being flogged and crucified, so be aware if you watch this with children. Watch it first for yourself and make the decision whether or not you want to show it to little ones.

But it is powerful! Your troubles will fade and disappear as you see what Jesus did for you on the cross and that He is risen from the dead and that He is real and heaven is real! This is a video to watch every day if not many times a day. It really puts our lives here on the planet earth in perspective.

Devotional Thoughts

"WORTHY IS THE LAMB THAT WAS SLAIN to receive power and riches and wisdom and might and honor and glory and blessing. To Him who sits on the throne, and to the Lamb, be blessing and honor and glory and dominion forever and ever."

All my troubles fade when I meditate on this verse. When I listen to the Revelation Song. When I think that He died for me, that He rose again, that He is real. And heaven is real. My heart sings for joy when I realize this! None of my circumstances has changed one iota, but I have incredible, deep, beautiful happiness that is a blessing beyond belief!

Day 4

Every created being will be singing this chorus out of the heart at the last days, including me. It will be an incredible joy bubbling out of me. I won't be able to stop it! I am barely able to stop it now!

Because Jesus is worthy of my adoration. He is worthy of my trust. He is the only being or thing that is. He possesses power, riches, wisdom, might, honor, glory, blessing.

And He will reign forever and ever.

Everything is His.

I need to give everything to Him.

Response

ALMIGHTY GOD, I GIVE YOU MY FEARS that are creeping up, the stress that I face on a daily basis, the doubt that I sometimes have that You will come through for me. You know what my family and I need. Please help me to trust in You, lean on You for Your power, riches, wisdom, might and honor and glory and blessing. I adore You, Lord Jesus. My troubles will fade in the light of Your glory. I love you!

Encouragement/Challenge

WHAT IS YOUR PERSPECTIVE? Will what you are worrying about matter in the light of eternity? Whom are you adoring? Sing the Revelation Song, watch the accompanying video, and praise God! Don't hold anything back!

Activity

WATCH A MOVIE ABOUT THE LIFE OF JESUS as a family. There are so many choices out there! We spend so much time entertaining ourselves through mindless shows, why not reinforce the image of Jesus as real in our lives and the lives of our children? Even if some of these movies (like *The Nativity Story*) are not completely historically accurate, it does show that Jesus is not some fairy tale. They were real events that changed history.

Prayer

OH MIGHTY GOD, we thank You that You are all powerful and You alone are worthy of our adoration! We praise You and we love You! Help us to have perspective and we thank You that no matter what our circumstances, we can truly have joy. Because You are our blessing! *In Jesus' Name, Amen.*

> "The LORD bless you, and keep you;
> The LORD make His face
> shine on you, And be gracious to you;
> The LORD lift up His
> countenance on you, And give you
> peace."
> —Numbers 6:25–26, *New American Standard Bible*

Prayer

Oh Faithful God, You are the great weaver of circumstances. You can take harm that is done to us and turn it for our good. We praise You that even in the midst of out of control circumstances that You are in control. *In Jesus' Name, Amen.*

Worship

"Forever God is Faithful"
Michael W. Smith

Scripture

Genesis 39

Genesis 39:5, *NASB*

It came about that from the time he made him overseer in his house and over all that he owned, the LORD blessed the Egyptian's house on account of Joseph; thus the LORD'S blessing was upon all that he owned, in the house and in the field.

 Day 5

What Does God Say About Blessings?

_____
_____
_____
_____
_____
_____
_____
_____
_____
_____

What Is My Response?

_____
_____
_____
_____
_____
_____
_____
_____
_____
_____

For Further Study

History of Joseph

Wikipedia gives some interesting facts about the history of Joseph, but you'll have to sift through the inherit cynicism and possible inaccuracy found in sites such as these. Here is the direct link:
https://en.wikipedia.org/wiki/Joseph_%28Bible%29

Devotional Thoughts

GOD BLESSED JOSEPH. Joseph faithfully took care of what He was given charge of and left the results to God. Even when circumstances turned against Joseph, he still kept faithfully taking care of all that was given him, and trusted God for the results, not knowing that his jail sentence would ultimately lead to saving his entire family and birth a nation, which would eventually bless the whole world. It was God who blessed.

Response

AGAIN I SEE THIS MESSAGE: God is faithful, therefore I need to faithfully complete the tasks I've been given and leave the results to God. No matter what my circumstances, I can rely on Him to see me through to the other side.

Like a recent dream I had—I was sliding down a steep mountain. A friend held my

Day 5

hand all the way down, and when I came to a bump or jump on the mountain, I would feel my friend's hand in mine and fly over the obstacles. At the bottom, I landed in a pool and was overwhelmed for a few seconds, but I came out the other side safe and joyful!

I've been sliding down many steep mountains, facing many challenges, and the whole way, God has held my hand. When the going has gotten rough, I have felt him squeeze a little harder and I fly over the obstacle. I must have landed or am near landing because lately I've felt that I've been drowning, but I know that I know that He will bring me safe and sound to the other side, joyful and blessed!

Encouragement/Challenge

WHAT CIRCUMSTANCES ARE YOU GOING THROUGH that you feel overwhelmed by? Take His hand and let Him guide you through these obstacles. Are you faithful with the tasks He has given you? Forget everything except obedience to Him. You will come out the other side blessed beyond belief!

Activity

HAVE YOUR CHILDREN STUDY THE STORY of Joseph and draw a picture of him with his many colored coat or any other favorite scene in the story.

Prayer

Sovereign God, You can take any circumstance and turn it into good for Your glory and good for all around us. No matter what we're going through, You are faithful. Just help us to be faithful and obedient to You each day of our lives *In Jesus' Name, Amen.*

"The LORD bless you,
and keep you;
The LORD make His face
shine on you,
And be gracious to you;
The LORD lift up His
countenance on you,
And give you peace."
—Numbers 6:25–26, *New American Standard Bible*

Blessings Journey Day 6

Prayer

Faithful Lord, we thank You for Your promises, that they are "yes" in Christ. We count on You with every fiber of our being. Help us to realize this and daily practice utter dependence on You. *In Jesus' Name, Amen.*

Worship

"Great is Thy Faithfulness"
Avalon

Scripture

2 Corinthians 1:12–24

2 Corinthians 1:15-20, *NASB*

In this confidence I intended at first to come to you, so that you might twice receive a blessing; that is, to pass your way into Macedonia, and again from Macedonia to come to you, and by you to be helped on my journey to Judea.

Therefore, I was not vacillating when I intended to do this, was I? Or what I purpose, do I purpose according to the flesh, so that with me there will be yes, yes and no, no at the same time?

But as God is faithful, our word to you is not yes and no.

For the Son of God, Christ Jesus, who was preached among you by us—by me and Silvanus and Timothy—was not yes and no, but is yes in Him.

For as many as are the promises of God, in Him they are yes; therefore also through Him is our Amen to the glory of God through us.

 Day 6

What Does God Say About Blessings?

_____
_____
_____
_____
_____
_____
_____
_____
_____

What Is My Response?

_____
_____
_____
_____
_____
_____
_____
_____

For Further Study

Map Out the Missionary Journeys of Paul Using Your Bible or Resources Online

You can find pretty good information by just Googling "Paul's missionary journeys." Go to the Images tab and you will find some great maps to explore!

Devotional Thoughts

THE PROMISES OF GOD IS A YES IN CHRIST JESUS. God is not double-minded, saying yes and no. He is faithful. This is to the glory of God. We are not to make our decisions in the flesh, but the Spirit is to guide us, as we trust Him to be faithful.

Response

I NEED TO COUNT ON HIM FOR THE CIRCUMSTANCES I am facing in my life today. I need to strive to make decisions in the Spirit, not the flesh, like the decision I made to work on this devotional instead of some other pressing projects that need to be finished immediately. He will redeem this time, because He doesn't say yes and no—He is faithful.

I need to instill this in my son, too, as we make a decision about a vehicle, whether to sell it for scrap or keep it to work on. This could be a special auto mechanic project for him. It's a lifeskill he needs to learn. But the biggest question is this: is he committed to working on it? He needs to learn that his yes needs to be

Day 6

yes, not "I don't know." The best way I can teach him this is to be a model of this important principle.

Encouragement/Challenge

WHAT ARE YOU DOUBTING GOD ABOUT? Just confess it and move on! Say, *"I believe, help me in my unbelief."* Read God's promises over and over again. Are you faithful to your promises as far as you are able? Practice only saying yes to those things you are fully committed to following through on.

Activity

STUDY THE LAND AND HISTORY OF TURKEY. Research the country's history, dominant religion, culture, and food. Have a culture day where you dress like someone in Turkey. Make it a festival with food, song, dance, and stories. Pray for the people in Turkey and support a missionary to Turkey.

Prayer

FAITHFUL GOD, thank You for all Your glorious promises, that You come through when You say You are coming through! Thank You for being a God we can count on no matter what our circumstances. Help us to remember this and to make decisions

Blessings Journey

in the Spirit, not in the flesh. *In Jesus' Name, Amen.*

"The LORD bless you,
and keep you;
The LORD make His face
shine on you,
And be gracious to
you;
The LORD lift up His
countenance on you,
And give you peace."
—Numbers 6:25–26, *New American Standard Bible*

Blessings Journey Day 7

Prayer

Amazing God, You can do so much more than we can ever ask or think! Thank You that You are uncontainable, beautiful, and blessed! *In Jesus' Name, Amen.*

Worship

"Indescribable"
Chris Tomlin

Scripture

Psalm 144

Psalm 144:1-2, *NASB*

Blessed be the LORD, my rock,
Who trains my hands for war,
And my fingers for battle;

My lovingkindness and my fortress,
My stronghold and my deliverer,
My shield and He in whom I take refuge,
Who subdues my people under me.

 Day 7

What Does God Say About Blessings?

_____
_____
_____
_____
_____
_____
_____
_____
_____

What Is My Response?

_____
_____
_____
_____
_____
_____
_____
_____

For Further Study

The Heart of Passion Mini-Series

I saw the tail end of this series on TV one night when I was working on this devotional. It is ***amazing!*** It will give you a fresh perspective on God's greatness.

Just search "Heart of Passion Mini Series" in YouTube by Louie Giglio or search for the four-part series on Amazon.

Devotional Thoughts

BLESSINGS ARE A TWO-WAY STREET. I bless God, I praise Him for who He is—a rock, my fortress, loving King, my deliverer, my shield in whom I take refuge. I acknowledge that I am nothing without Him, that I need Him, that He is the one who trains me for "war," He rescues me. I ask boldly for Him to come down, to fight for me, to rescue and deliver me from "aliens"—those who are false and full of deceit. I ask Him boldly that my son would be a grown-up plant, that our barns (bank accounts) would be full, that we would be productive and our work would multiply, be fruitful. And bless many, many people. And all this without loss. And so I ask because my God is my Lord and great blessings are a benefit from such a give and give relationship.

Day 7

Response

I NEED TO KEEP BOLDLY ASKING HIM FOR MY NEEDS, WANTS, AND DESIRES; for a full bank account, yes, but so much more, the big dreams He has put on my heart, for instance that my son would be a "grown-up plant." But while I pray boldly, I need to even more boldly praise Him, singing a new song of adoration and love. I need to look to Him as my deliverer, my redeemer. The uncontainable God who can do abundantly beyond whatever I could ask or think (Ephesians 3:20).

Encouragement/Challenge

WHAT ARE YOU BELIEVING GOD FOR? Is your God limited or is He indescribable? What are your dreams? What are the dreams that He's put on your heart, for you, your children, your family... Take some time and meditate on God's greatness and then pray boldly for these dreams.

Activity

STUDY ASTRONOMY. The pictures of the universe through the Hubble telescope is a great place to start.

Prayer

Wondrous Lord, we praise You for Your beauty, blessing, and glory. You can do the seemingly impossible! Help us to open our eyes to Your incredible power and dream the dreams that You have laid on our hearts. Help us to reach for Your abundance and true riches in glory. *In Jesus' Name, Amen.*

"The LORD bless you,
and keep you;
The LORD make His face
shine on you,
And be gracious to you;
The LORD lift up His
countenance on you,
And give you peace."
—Numbers 6:25–26, *New American Standard Bible*

Prayer

Thank you, Lord, that You give power to Your people, as well as incredible love. Help us to live in that power and love day by day! *In Jesus' Name, Amen.*

Worship

"More Love, More Power"

Scripture

Joshua 17

Joshua 17:14, *NASB*

Then the sons of Joseph spoke to Joshua, saying, "Why have you given me only one lot and one portion for an inheritance, since I am a numerous people whom the Lord has thus far blessed?"

 Day 8

What Does God Say About Blessings?

_____
_____
_____
_____
_____
_____
_____
_____
_____

What Is My Response?

_____
_____
_____
_____
_____
_____
_____
_____

For Further Study

Study Ephesians 6:10–18, the Section About the Armor of God

This is a prayer I like to say on a daily basis. In fact, I find PraiseMoves and Power Promises by Laurette Willis a very joyful way to start the day! This passage is foundational in her programs.

Devotional Thoughts

OBSTACLES. What are they to the Lord's people whom He has blessed? The advances of the enemy, the unforgiving terrain—they were surmountable because God had given Joseph's people great power.

What are obstacles I face? Personally—disorganization, lack of finances, lack of significant friendships, energy... Nationally—this economic downturn, the threatening socialism in this country...

Since originally writing this devotional thought, God has brought us a long ways, especially with finances. Our biggest obstacles now are these: our son's lack of functionality as a result of high-functioning Autism and my lack of energy. Oh yes, clutter and disorganization are still factors!

But if God is with me, all these obstacles are surmountable. Do I believe it?

Day 8

Response

REALIZE THAT GOD HAS GIVEN ME GREAT POWER. Keep praying for abundance, for blessing, engage in spiritual warfare, and keep doing the things that God has called me to do.

Encouragement/Challenge

WHAT ARE OBSTACLES THAT YOU FACE? Take on the battle by "facing the giants" in your life. The most important thing you can do is to go to God in prayer and to pray with others. Spend some time engaged in spiritual warfare. Do not let the enemy defeat you, but keep fighting by putting on the whole armor of God. And never forget that He loves you, more than you can ever imagine. So much that He died for you so you could live.

Activity

HAVE YOUR KIDS CREATE the parts of God's armor out of cardboard or some other material. Then spend some time in prayer specifically to engage in spiritual warfare. But be sure to ask for protection in Jesus' name. Satan doesn't like it when we fight back, and he is a bully to the weak, especially our children.

Prayer

O<small>H LOVING AND POWERFUL</small> G<small>OD</small>, thank You that You gave us power to overcome obstacles. Thank You that nothing is impossible with Your Son. Help us to continually worship You with all our hearts, souls, and minds, and protect us from the evil one as we keep believing in Your willingness and ability to bless us extravagantly. *In Jesus' Name, Amen.*

> "The LORD bless you,
> and keep you;
> The LORD make His face
> shine on you,
> And be gracious to you;
> The LORD lift up His
> countenance on you,
> And give you peace."
>
> —Numbers 6:25–26, *New American Standard Bible*

Blessings Journey Day 9

Prayer

Thank you, Lord, that in You alone is our life! Thank You for paying the ultimate price so we could live. Help us to be a blessing to others, even if we are being insulted. Help us to keep looking to You even when we are suffering for "the sake of righteousness." *In Jesus' Name, Amen.*

Worship

"In Christ Alone"
Adrienne Liesching and Geoff Moore

Scripture

1 Peter 3:8–22

Blessings Journey

1 Peter 3:14, *NASB*

But even if you should suffer for the sake of righteousness, you are blessed. And do not fear their intimidation, and do not be troubled.

 Day 9

What Does God Say About Blessings?

_____
_____
_____
_____
_____
_____
_____
_____
_____
_____

What Is My Response?

_____
_____
_____
_____
_____
_____
_____
_____

For Further Study

Study the Meaning of Baptism in Scripture, Both in the Old and New Testaments

Bible Gateway's dictionary has some interesting things to say. Here's the link:

https://www.biblegateway.com/resources/dictionaries/dict_meaning.php?source=3&wid=S7154

Devotional Thoughts

I WILL NEVER BE TRULY HARMED if I am proved zealous for what is good. In fact, I am blessed even if I should suffer for the sake of righteousness.

My family and I have been experiencing this in great detail lately. When we decided to move from our old house into one that had facilities "all there." Primarily because the move would be best for our son, who has special needs. We prayed and prayed before the move, and before we decided to turn the old house into a vacation rental, our heart's cry was, *"Where do you want us, God?"* We stepped out in faith, moved, remodeled our old house and turned it into a vacation rental.

But then the economy tanked and at the same time our old neighbors treated us extremely unkindly. They did not like our decision to turn it into a vacation rental and instead of discussing their concerns with us, they yelled at us, turned us into city code for nonexistent issues, and collaborated with city government to end our business. This stung deeply and we suffered with having to pay two mortgages with very little income to cover the expense.

I used to ask, *"Why God?"* Why would this happen when we went out of our way

 Day 9

to be where You wanted us to be, which resulted in our decision to homeschool our son which resulted in recognizing the special needs we have in our family and the wisdom to address them?

Then, after we put our old house up for short sale, the truth of it stunned me. God led us out of that house because He knew the housing prices would plummet, and if we had stayed, we would have nothing! We would be stuck with horrible neighbors and a house not suitable for homeschooling and not suitable for our special needs!

What a blessing! We have a beautiful home, and though it is hard to keep up with all the financial demands because of the domino effect of the second house, we are grateful that God brought us here! He delivered us from a bad situation and we are looking to Him for guidance in how to recover our finances after such a hard blow. Above all, we need to keep fear at bay and keep setting our hearts on Him.

And since this original entry into my journal, God has blessed us with a growing architectural business and my parents helped us figure out a way we could keep our home. I am blessed beyond belief for such caring, wonderful parents! Dreams that we once thought out of reach are coming true, like getting our son much-needed therapy and replacing our vehicles. But most importantly, our hearts are transformed and we have more confidence in God that He is the one who provides.

Response

Do NOT FEAR the neighbor's intimidation. Do not be troubled. Keep praying blessings over the neighbors who hurt me, despite my feelings.

Sanctify Christ as Lord in my heart, ready to make defense to everyone who asks me to give an account for the hope that is in me, yet with gentleness and reverence.

Why? Because Christ died for my sins, once for all, in order that He might bring me to God, having been put to death in the flesh, but made alive in the Spirit.

This is the crux of the Blessed *not* Stressed lifestyle. Not giving into the fear all around me, doing what is right no matter what. I will be shining with true hope and others will notice. I need to be ready to give an account for the hope I have which is the Lord sanctified in my heart as LORD. I do this because He died for my sins so that He might bring me to God. I am dead in the flesh and alive in the Spirit.

Encouragement/Challenge

IS FEAR DOMINATING YOUR LIFE, controlling you? How is fear keeping you from really stepping out in faith? What is your response when evil is done to you? Hurling insults or hurling blessings?

Activity

SPEND SOME TIME AS A FAMILY volunteering at a community shelter, food bank, hospital, or ministry. Show them that through Christ, we can be hands and feet to the gospel, especially to the unloved, the rejected, and the forgotten.

Day 9

Prayer

OUR WONDERFUL LORD, thank You that because of You our hearts do not have to be troubled. That when we look to You, our fears disappear because You are incredibly powerful and loving. Help us to sanctify You in our hearts, to always set You apart as Lord of our lives and of everything we have and are. *In Jesus' Name, Amen.*

> "The LORD bless you,
> and keep you;
> The LORD make His face
> shine on you,
> And be gracious to you;
> The LORD lift up His
> countenance on you,
> And give you peace."
> —Numbers 6:25–26, *New American Standard Bible*

Prayer

Thank You, our Lord King, that You bless the seeds that we sow generously and You inspire noble plans in us. Help us to walk in integrity and instead of giving into fear, lead us to step out in faith. *In Jesus' Name, Amen.*

Worship

"Shout to the North"
Delirious

Scripture

Isaiah 32

Isaiah 32:20, *NASB*

How blessed will you be, you who sow beside all waters,
Who let out freely the ox and the donkey.

 Day 10

What Does God Say About Blessings?

What Is My Response?

For Further Study

Study Ecclesiastes 11
This chapter has some important nuggets to chew on regarding financial security, work ethic, and the fleeting nature of youth.

Devotional Thoughts

"BUT THE NOBLE WOMAN DEVISES *noble plans; and by noble plans she stands." —my paraphrase.*

This chapter describes both millennial blessings and horrifying famine. One is the present or near future, the other in years to come. Yet there's this interesting verse that caught my eye. In the midst of these trying times what is a woman to do? Yes, put on sackcloth and ashes and mourn, but I like this idea of devising noble plans. If I live by integrity, while everyone else is being swept away, I will be firmly planted because I followed my principles. And instead of shutting down in fear, I asked for God's guidance, developed a vision, and sowed my seed with generosity. The result will be blessings.

So this was the beginning of amazing transformation in our lives. Because of the inspiration of this verse, I made a noble plan. I decided that I would learn as much as I could about Internet marketing and create online programs to help people achieve financial independence. I invested in my first Internet course, and from the knowledge gained I created my program **Brand Identity Quest.** *My husband was the first one to take that course and he used it to develop his business, Essential*

 **Day 10**

Pillar Architecture. Now he works from home full-time and we are actively growing that business. It is achieving for us financial independence. Now I am taking my course, revamping it, and getting ready to help many more families achieve their financial independence. I also turned it into a homeschooling curriculum.

Response

Let nobility and honor guide me. Practice integrity. Keep sowing generously the seeds that God has given me, using the talents and gifts that came from Him for His glory. Make my plans and walk in integrity.

At the time of this original writing, I decided to pursue a home study course on Internet marketing. This to me was a noble plan, to learn how to make money online so I could contribute to our family's needs, help market my husband's architectural business, and lay the groundwork for my son to have the choice to be an entrepreneur when he grows up. I have stuck by this plan, and I have learned a lot! In fact, writing and promoting this 31-Day Blessings Journey is a direct result of that conviction that took place over a year ago. I was experiencing a great deal of stress then and I will tell you at times the stress had not lessened at all. In fact, our stress had gotten worse. But having these noble plans and seeing myself as the daughter of the King enabled me to keep going on despite the problems we faced. And I know that the seeds I have been planting will grow up someday soon into beautiful plants!

Encouragement/Challenge

What is your response in these turbulent times or when you are faced with overwhelming stress? Is it to flee, to react in fear? Instead of running from the stress, devise a plan with God's help and inspiration and stand by it. Seek Him for guidance and remember that you are a child of the King. Keep sowing generously and wait for the blessing to come.

Activity

Plant some seeds together. Have your child rake, hoe, and sow the seed. Have her water it until it grows mature. This can be an indoor or outdoor activity, depending on the time of year. Let your child choose the kind of plant to grow. Read *The Secret Garden* together and give your child his own plot of earth to tend!

Prayer

Dearest Lord, we praise You that true growth comes from You. We lay our plans at Your feet, trusting that in You they will be truly noble. Help us to live generously and live faithfully. *In Jesus' Name, Amen.*

 Day 10

"The LORD bless you,
and keep you;
The LORD make His face
shine on you,
And be gracious to you;
The LORD lift up His
countenance on you,
And give you peace."
—Numbers 6:25–26, *New American Standard Bible*

Blessings Journey Day 11

Prayer

Dear Lord Jesus, thank You that You came to serve and not to be served. Thank You that You know where You came from and where You're going. Help us to have a different kind of confidence, a God confidence, and to take care of those You have given us. *In Jesus' Name, Amen.*

Worship

"The Steadfast Love of the Lord Never Ceases"

Scripture

John 13

John 13:14–20, *NASB*

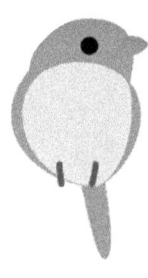

"If I then, the Lord and the Teacher, washed your feet, you also ought to wash one another's feet. For I gave you an example that you also should do as I did to you. Truly, truly, I say to you, a slave is not greater than his master, nor is one who is sent greater than the one who sent him. If you know these things, you are blessed if you do them. I do not speak of all of you. I know the ones I have chosen; but it is that the Scripture may be fulfilled, 'He who eats My bread has lifted up his heel against Me.' From now on I am telling you before it comes to pass, so that when it does occur, you may believe that I am He. Truly, truly, I say to you, he who receives whomever I send receives Me; and he who receives Me receives Him who sent Me."

 Day 11

What Does God Say About Blessings?

_____
_____
_____
_____
_____
_____
_____
_____
_____

What Is My Response?

_____
_____
_____
_____
_____
_____
_____
_____

For Further Study

Study Lamentations
This famous passage is one to sink your teeth into! God's compassions are new every day! Study this passage and think about examples of how these words have been manifested in your own life.
OR Study the cultural ramifications of foot-washing in the times Jesus lived.

Devotional Thoughts

JESUS KNEW WHERE HE WAS COMING FROM and He knows where He was going that Maundy Thursday night. He had absolute confidence in himself—actually He had more than that, He had God-confidence. Even knowing He would be betrayed, beaten, and killed, He was still faithful to love the ones who were given to Him on this earth. He was an example of this type of love, and He is an example for me today.

Response

I HAVE BEEN GIVEN MY HUSBAND AND SON. I have not always been faithful in loving them. And now I see what I lack: God-confidence.

When I originally wrote this entry in March of 2009, I had had a really bad day. I was feeling like God had abandoned me in the overwhelming stress I was experiencing. Deep down I believed that God was just like my earthly Dad, a Dad I love very much but sometimes—because he is not outwardly affectionate and instead is a man

Day 11

of action, not words—it seemed to me that he didn't care. That was my perception, not reality. But because of this misperception, this is a scar I've born from early childhood and God has brought me a long ways to overcome my wrong interpretation.

Since that time, I have come to see that my earthly father truly does care for me. He has been a vivid picture to me of the love of the Heavenly Father. It was my wrong interpretation of his reluctance to show affection that caused the struggle.

This is what I wrote on March 4, 2009:

I really believe God has given up on me.

Like my father, he couldn't care less. I'm all on my own to figure it out. He shows no affection to me at all. Logically, I know my Dad does this because he is extremely left-brained and doesn't show affection except through actions.

But still, I struggle with abandonment issues. I have to go it alone. I have to figure it out for myself.

Last night I felt like giving up.

Let Travis and Sam figure dinner out on their own because I am a failure as a wife and mother. But I couldn't bear to see them suffer, not even one of my "flock"— my animals.

I couldn't starve them or ignore the cry of the animals, I can't abandon them like that.

So here I am again today. With a new chance. His mercies are new every morning.

I can't do it on my own. I need help. I need God confidence.

Encouragement/Challenge

WHAT KIND OF CONFIDENCE DO YOU HAVE? Confidence in yourself or confidence in God? Do you have any confidence at all? Who has God given you to take care of? What is your attitude about that? What childhood issues have caused you to believe the lie that God has abandoned you and doesn't care about you? Work on these issues and study the truth until it is deep in your heart!

Activity

TAKE CARE OF ONE ANOTHER. For the day, encourage each family member to serve one another. For instance, wash each others' dinner plates, make each others' beds, clean each others' rooms. At night, celebrate with a special meal and wash each others' feet just as Jesus washed the feet of His disciples. Discuss why foot-washing was such an important task in Biblical times. What comparable chore exists today?

Prayer

FAITHFUL GOD, we praise You that Your mercies are new every day! Thank You for caring so deeply about us. Help us to trust in You more and more each day. *In Jesus' Name, Amen.*

Day 11

"The LORD bless you,
and keep you;
The LORD make His face
shine on you,
And be gracious to you;
The LORD lift up His
countenance on you,
And give you peace."

—Numbers 6:25–26, *New American Standard Bible*

Prayer

Dear Lord Jesus, thank You that You are worthy of our trust and worthy of our obedience. Help us to love, trust, and obey You with all our hearts. *In Jesus' Name, Amen.*

Worship

"Trust and Obey"
Hillsong Kids

Scripture

Deuteronomy 28:1–14

Deuteronomy 28:1–2, *NASB*

"Now it shall be, if you diligently obey the Lord your God, being careful to do all His commandments which I command you today, the Lord your God will set you high above all the nations of the earth. All these blessings will come upon you and overtake you if you obey the Lord your God."

 Day 12

What Does God Say About Blessings?

_____
_____
_____
_____
_____
_____
_____
_____
_____

What Is My Response?

_____
_____
_____
_____
_____
_____
_____
_____

For Further Study

Study 1 Samuel 13:1–15
Study this incident in King Saul's life. How did not obeying the Lord whole-heartedly effect his life? What would have happened if he *had* obeyed God with all his heart?

Devotional Thoughts

HOW DO BLESSINGS COME ABOUT? By obeying the Lord my God, by being careful to do all His commandments. By walking in His ways. In other words, having whole-hearted devotion to Him, not to turn aside to the right or to the left, or get distracted by other gods in my life.

If I do this, He promises blessings:

1) Set me high above the people of the earth; 2) All blessings shall come upon me and overtake me; 3) Blessed wherever I choose to dwell; 4) My offspring and my produce and my herds will increase; 5) My kitchen will be blessed; 6) Comings and goings; 7) Enemies will be defeated and run away; 8) Blessings will be upon my work; 9) Established as a holy person to Himself; 10) A witness to others, that I am *called by the name of the Lord;* 11) Abounding in prosperity in my offspring, my assets, my business; 12) My work will be fruitful and I will lend, not borrow; 13) I will be a leader, above the fray.

Day 12

Response

WHAT ARE THE GODS THAT DISTRACT ME? Fear of rejection, seeking approval, self-hatred, thinking that God makes trash, relying on myself or others rather than God. I need to continually work on repentance to bring me back in balance with God. The more stress I have the more I realize I depend on God for everything. It's not easy waiting and it's not easy believing that prosperity will come, that anything will change. I have to continue to walk with Him in whole-hearted devotion, no matter what the hardships or struggles I face. I can't fix my eyes on those bumps in the road that come up, but I need to be looking up to God.

Encouragement/Challenge

WHAT ARE THE "GODS" THAT DISTRACT YOU? What in our culture has become an idol to you and your family and is preventing you from being whole-heartedly devoted to God? Take a moment individually as a family to ascertain what these are and come up with a plan of action to get rid of them. But don't merely get rid of an idol, replace it with some form of God worship!

For instance, I felt that network TV was a distracting idol to me. I would naturally default toward watching the garbage on it because there was nothing else available. I became convicted that I didn't want such pollution in my house, so instead of just getting rid of it, I bought SkyAngel, a Christian-based Internet TV service. Additionally, I did not get converter boxes when television went from analog

to digital. Then after a time when SkyAngel wasn't working for us (the cost wasn't worth the benefits and unfortunately they went out of business because many people recognized this), we just watch Netflix, Amazon Prime, and DVDs.

To me, watching television is relaxing and helps my brain to wind down. I wanted to fill that brain with good things! I didn't merely get rid of the habit, I replaced it with a good one!

Now your idols will look different; everyone is unique, so here is your chance to reflect:

Our "gods"

_____
_____
_____

Our Plan Of Action To Get Rid Of Them

_____
_____
_____

What Will I Replace Them With?

_____
_____
_____
_____

 # Day 12

Activity

As a family, pretend you are walking on a tightrope. If you have a balance beam or something safe to walk across even better yet! Make signs: on the far side of the beam or rope is God. Underneath and to the sides are the gods of this world. Have family members shout at the person walking across to try to distract them. Those who can cross without losing their balance or going to their right or left are the winners.

Prayer

Holy Lord, we praise You for pouring out Your blessings on us, in all facets of our lives. Help us to keep depending on You for everything we have and are, to love You with all our hearts, souls, and minds. *In Jesus' Name, Amen.*

> "The LORD bless you, and keep you;
> The LORD make His face
> shine on you, And be gracious
> to you; The LORD lift up His
> countenance on you, And
> give you peace."
>
> —Numbers 6:25–26, *New American Standard Bible*

Prayer

Heavenly Father, we thank You that You give us the strength to persevere. Help us to rely on You alone. *In Jesus' Name, Amen.*

Worship

"Beautiful One"
Tim Hughes

Scripture

James 5:1–12

James 5:11, *NASB*

We count those blessed who endured. You have heard of the endurance of Job and have seen the outcome of the Lord's dealings, that the Lord is full of compassion and is merciful.

 Day 13

What Does God Say About Blessings?

What Is My Response?

For Further Study

Do a Topical Bible study on How God Views the Rich

1) Look up passages in the Bible that say rich, wealthy, or whatever synonym you can think of.

2) Go to http://www.biblegateway.com and insert those words into the search form.

3) Keep a notebook or journal and for each passage ask, *"What does God say about the rich?"* and *"What is my response?"* This is the easiest form of Topical Bible Study, although you can make it more advanced by observing who, what, when, why, and how facts of each passage, asking difficult questions, and choosing key words and defining them.

Devotional Thoughts

GOD HEARS THE CRY OF THE RIPPED-OFF. Those who fatten their hearts with luxuries will pay in the end.

That means a lot to me at this time when we have been so exploited and our finances have been brought to ruin by those who led us down a primrose path.

It is also a reminder not to treat people like this.

Blessed am I when I endure. Patience is key. It's essential. I have to look to God for the nourishing of my labors, for the eventual harvest.

Not easy in these turbulent times with so many needs hitting me at once, and where there seems to be no relief in site.

But one thing I know: each day I need to ask Him a simple question: *What are*

Day 13

Your callings for me today? If I obey Him in this simple prayer, all will work out and blessings will be the result.

Response

UNTIL THIS HARVEST, I need to be patient and strengthen my heart, for the coming of the Lord is at hand.

I am blessed when I endure and trust God for the outcome. Because He is full of compassion and mercy.

This is not easy and I have good days and bad days. Days when I'm sure everything will work out all right. Days when I don't see how anything in my situation could ever change. But no matter what, I need to be a person of integrity, sticking by my word and doing the things God has given me to do. Again, it's doing that and then resting, trusting Him for the results.

And I have seen results! Many things that seemed impossible have come true. It's worth the wait and agony!

Encouragement/Challenge

WHAT LIFE STRESSES ARE YOU HAVING TO ENDURE? What is God calling you to do? Ask God this every morning and then be faithful as far as you are able to answer those callings. Then rest and leave the results up to God.

What Are You Calling Me To Today, Lord?

_____
_____
_____

Activity

PURCHASE A VEGETABLE OR FRUIT PLANT, like those upside-down tomato or strawberry plants. Together as a family choose it, plant it, water it, fertilize it, and then harvest it, enjoying the nourishment you received from it. Relate this experience to James 5.

Prayer

HEAVENLY FATHER, thank You that You will be coming soon and then You will wipe every tear, every heartache. Help us to persevere and lean on you no matter what our circumstances. *In Jesus' Name, Amen.*

> "The LORD bless you, and keep you;
> The LORD make His face shine on you,
> And be gracious to you; The LORD lift
> up His countenance on you, And give
> you peace."
>
> –Numbers 6:25–26, *New American Standard Bible*

Prayer

Dear Heavenly Father, thank You for blessing us with children. They are a gift from You. Help us to be wise parents and to be models of Your love. *In Jesus' Name, Amen.*

Worship

"Behold What Manner of Love"

Scripture

Psalms 127

Psalm 127:3–5, *The Message*

Don't you see that children are God's best gift?
the fruit of the womb his generous legacy?
Like a warrior's fistful of arrows
are the children of a vigorous youth.
Oh, how blessed are you parents,
with your quivers full of children!
Your enemies don't stand a chance against you;
you'll sweep them right off your doorstep.

 Day 14

What Does God Say About Blessings?

_____
_____
_____
_____
_____
_____
_____
_____
_____

What Is My Response?

_____
_____
_____
_____
_____
_____
_____
_____
_____

For Further Study

Study Children and Parenting in the Bible
Who is responsible for teaching them? What does the Scripture say about discipline? What happens when a child is hurt? How does God feel about that? Read passages from the Old Testament and New Testament. Get together with other parents and study the Scriptures.

Devotional Thoughts

He gives to His beloved even in my sleep. He builds the house, he guards the city, it is He who labors. It is He who gives the gift of children. Pregnancy/children are not a burden, but a reward. Blessings come with having a lot of these rewards.

Response

I think Sam by himself is a "quiver full." He is a handful. But he too is a huge blessing. Sam is the fruit of my womb, my reward, not a punishment. But I can't do it alone—I am dependent on God. And if He wills, He can bring me another fruit of my womb. It's totally in His hands.

On another note, do I believe I am God's beloved? How would I act if I believed it? Would I labor so much? Would I build and guard on my own?

This is the thought to apply—I am God's beloved.

Day 14

Encouragement/Challenge

If YOU ARE A PARENT, during those times of frustration (and they will come!) remember that your children are a reward. They are God's gift to you. Treat them like the treasures they are. Accept them for who they are, not who you want them to be. If you do not have children, consider coming alongside parents. A church setting is a great place to do this. Volunteer to be a Sunday School teacher or youth counselor. Also, for everyone, ask yourself the question, *"What if you believed that you are God's beloved?"* How would you act differently?

Activity

GO TO AN ARCHERY RANGE and learn how to shoot a bow and arrow. Discuss with your children what an arrow is, what a quiver full is and how those objects relate to this Psalm.

Prayer

DEAR LORD JESUS, thank You for all Your glorious promises, that You come through when You say You are coming through! Thank You for being a God we can count on no matter what our circumstances. Help us to remember this and to make decisions in the Spirit, not in the flesh. *In Jesus' Name, Amen.*

Blessings Journey

"The LORD bless you,
and keep you;
The LORD make His face
shine on you,
And be gracious to you;
The LORD lift up His
countenance on you,
And give you peace."

—Numbers 6:25–26, *New American Standard Bible*

Prayer

Our Dearest Lord, we love You with all our hearts, souls, and minds. Help us to be continually wholly devoted to You! *In Jesus' Name, Amen.*

Worship

"Love the Lord"
Lincoln Brewster

Scripture

1 Corinthians 10:14–21

1 Corinthians 10:14, *The Message*

So, my very dear friends, when you see people reducing God to something they can use or control, get out of their company as fast as you can.

 Day 15

What Does God Say About Blessings?

_____
_____
_____
_____
_____
_____
_____
_____
_____
_____

What Is My Response?

_____
_____
_____
_____
_____
_____
_____
_____
_____
_____

For Further Study

Study the Significance of Communion in the Scriptures
Why is communion important to God? How does He use it to bless us? What should our attitude be when we take communion? I'm sure you can come up with many more questions for this vital part of Christian life!

Devotional Thoughts

You can't participate in idolatry of the world and at the same time share in the "cup of blessing which we bless." You can't have a foot in the blessing world and the cursing world. God is a jealous God and He wants all of us.

Response

For me, I need to limit by exposure to network news. Fear and intimidation is what the demons are spreading through mainstream media, as well as chaos and the idolatry of looking to the government for saving us, for daily bread.
Instead, I need to partake in God and in the blessings of His fellowship.

Day 15

Encouragement/Challenge

Are you trying to live in both worlds? Both blessings from God and curses from the world? Are you trying to manipulate God into an idol that you can control? Spend some time with Jesus and determine to let go of your idols, giving your whole heart to Him.

Activity

For one night this week, instead of watching regular television or cable, get together as a family and sing praise songs together. Better yet, start a jam session. My family and I went to a bluegrass gospel jam session one night and it was fantastic! Got our minds off our troubles and our son got interested in playing the guitar!

Prayer

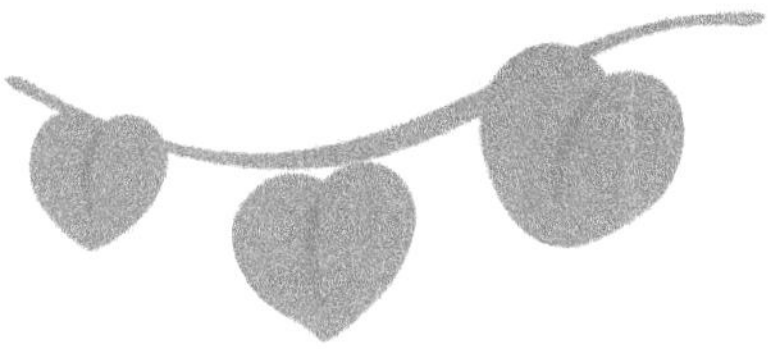

Dear Lord Jesus, thank You for Your blessings and that You are a jealous God, wanting our whole hearts. Help us to love You with everything we have and are. *In Jesus' Name, Amen.*

Blessings Journey

"The LORD bless you,
and keep you;
The LORD make His face
shine on you,
And be gracious to you;
The LORD lift up His
countenance on you,
And give you peace."

–Numbers 6:25–26, *New American Standard Bible*

Prayer

Our Blessed Lord, we thank You for the gift of Your son, Jesus Christ. We thank You for all the blessings You bestow on our lives. Help us to pass on these blessings to others so they can see Your glory! *In Jesus' Name, Amen.*

Worship

"The Choirboys—The Lord Bless You and Keep You"
Composed by John Rutter

or for a more modern song, one of my favorites is **"Shine, Jesus, Shine"**

Scripture

Numbers 6:22–27

Numbers 6:24–26, *The Message*

God bless you and keep you,

God smile on you and gift you,

*God look you full in the face
and make you prosper.*

 Day 16

What Does God Say About Blessings?

_____
_____
_____
_____
_____
_____
_____
_____
_____

What Is My Response?

_____
_____
_____
_____
_____
_____
_____
_____
_____

For Further Study

Learn More About Jewish Roots
Learn more about the Jewish roots and perspective of saying blessings through this interesting blog written by a work at home mom who lives in Jerusalem:

http://www.families.com/blog/blessed-are-youthe-significance-of-blessings-in-judaism

Devotional Thoughts

THIS IS AN EXTREMELY IMPORTANT PRAYER. God instituted it for the priests to say over the people, and God promised that His name would be on the people upon saying this prayer and that He would confirm it by blessing them.

The thought occurred to me: Is this just a prayer for ministers, like our pastor who prays this every Sunday before we are dismissed from church?

No! We are all called to the royal priesthood as disciples of Christ!

This blessing needs to be front and center in daily life, said over myself, my family, my friends, my business...

This is a huge key to transforming my stress into blessings—to more than surviving through hard times but experiencing thriving prosperity because of the hard times.

Day 16

Response

MEMORIZE THIS PRAYER AND USE IT OFTEN! Since writing this entry, I have said this prayer several times. It has helped me through days when my mood has been sad and life's challenges seemed impossible to overcome. I'm not through the woods yet, but I have a sense that saying this prayer over every aspect of my life is a huge mood lifter. A very wholesome anti-depressant indeed!

And it has been! As I've described on previous pages, the Lord has brought us a long ways!

Encouragement/Challenge

MEMORIZE THIS PRAYER AND SAY IT OFTEN, EVEN DAILY. Bless your children and say this prayer at night before they go to bed! Learn to say blessings over everything and everyone in your lives! Now watch to see how your burdens are lifted and your joy is increased! Even make a journal of it and log every time you sense an answer to this prayer.

Activity

MAKE A CARD FOR SOMEONE YOU KNOW is going through a hard time. Write this verse in it and send it to them. This can be a great family project. Pray this verse over

them. You can also use this idea to send cards to soldiers serving our country abroad.

Prayer

DEAREST HEAVENLY FATHER, we praise You that You are peace and that You sent the Prince of Peace to die in our place. We do humbly ask that You would make Your face to shine upon us, that You would keep us in Your love, and You would make us prosper. *In Jesus' Name, Amen.*

"The LORD bless you,
and keep you;
The LORD make His face
shine on you,
And be gracious to you;
The LORD lift up His
countenance on you,
And give you peace."
—Numbers 6:25–26, *New American Standard Bible*

Prayer

Dear Lord, You are our blessed hope and we thank You for saving us. Help us to wait eagerly for the glorious appearing of Your Son. *In Jesus' Name, Amen.*

Worship

"Song of Hope"
Robbie Seay Band

"Blessed Be Your Name"
Matt Redman

Scripture

Titus 2:11–15

Titus 2:11–13, *NASB*

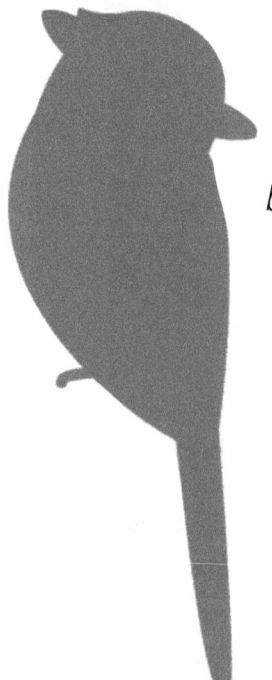

For the grace of God has appeared, bringing salvation to all men, instructing us to deny ungodliness and worldly desires and to live sensibly, righteously and godly in the present age, looking for the blessed hope and the appearing of the glory of our great God and Savior, Christ Jesus.

 Day 17

What Does God Say About Blessings?

_____
_____
_____
_____
_____
_____
_____
_____

What Is My Response?

_____
_____
_____
_____
_____
_____
_____
_____

For Further Study

Study the Word "Sanctification"

What does it mean? How does it apply to our daily lives? What are the biblical texts that speak about this process of becoming more like Jesus? What do you need before you can be sanctified? (Salvation.) What happens when Jesus appears and we are resurrected? (Glorification.)

Devotional Thoughts

WHAT IS THE PURPOSE OF MY LIFE? To look for the blessed hope and appearing of the glory of my great God and savior Jesus Christ who gave Himself up for me that He might redeem me from every lawless deed and purify Himself a person for His own possession, zealous for good deeds.

And until He appears? The grace of God appeared long ago and in my heart. He brought salvation to me. He instructs me to:
- Deny ungodliness and worldly desires.
- Live sensibly, righteously, and godly in the present age.

Response

THESE THINGS I AM TO LIVE AND THEN SPEAK and exhort and reprove with all authority letting no one disregard me.

So every decision I make needs to be brought to this light:

Day 17

- What is the purpose of...
- What (or whom) am I looking for?
- Where is the grace of God in this?
- Am I denying or accepting ungodliness in this decision?
- Will I be living sensibly, righteously, and godly if I make this decision?
- Once I make this decision, will it be an opportunity to speak and exhort and reprove with all authority, letting no one disregard me? These things I am to live and then speak and exhort and reprove with all authority letting no one disregard me.

Encouragement/Challenge

WHAT ARE YOU HOPING FOR? What is your life purpose? Look at the above decisions list and think about your decisions in light of this Scripture.

Activity

READ REVELATION 1:13–16, the description of Jesus. Imagine seeing Him in all His glory and have your children draw a picture with the passage as inspiration.

Prayer

Our Blessed God, thank You that You will come again soon in glory. Help us to be ready for Your arrival and to wait eagerly for Your appearing. *In Jesus' Name, Amen.*

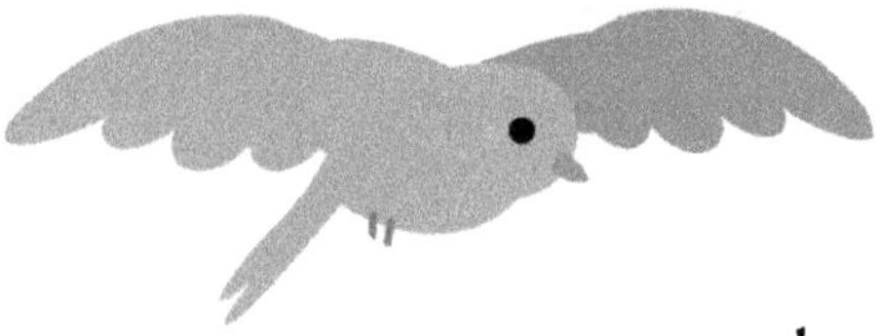

"The LORD bless you,
and keep you;
The LORD make His face
shine on you,
And be gracious to you;
The LORD lift up His
countenance on you,
And give you peace."

—Numbers 6:25–26, *New American Standard Bible*

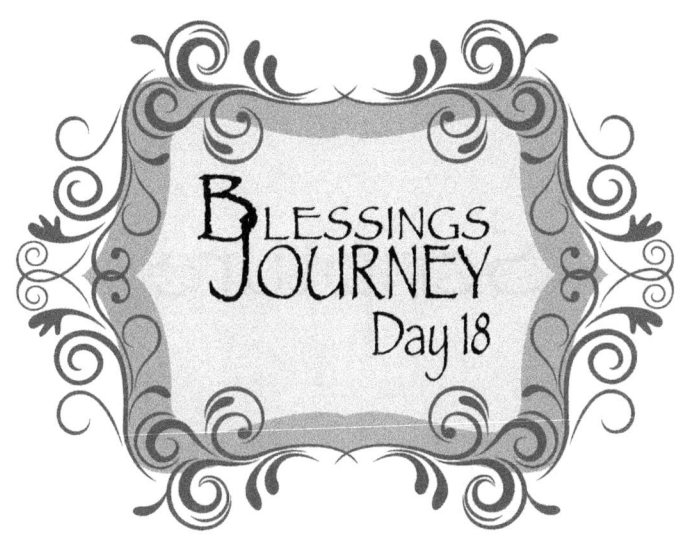

Prayer

O Precious Lord, thank You for Your abounding joy and Your enduring beauty. Help us to seek after You with our whole hearts! *In Jesus' Name, Amen.*

Worship

"Sing Hallelujah"
This song has almost a Jewish sound to it and has some beautiful scenery shots. It's based on Psalm 95. I really liked it. It's very different!

Here is the link:
https://www.youtube.com/watch?v=xBMaUeeqV1c

Scripture

Isaiah 65:1–16

Isaiah 65:16, *NASB*

*Because he who is blessed in the earth
Will be blessed by the God of truth;
And he who swears in the earth
Will swear by the God of truth;
Because the former troubles are forgotten,
And because they are hidden from My sight!*

 Day 18

What Does God Say About Blessings?

_____
_____
_____
_____
_____
_____
_____
_____
_____

What Is My Response?

_____
_____
_____
_____
_____
_____
_____
_____
_____
_____
_____

For Further Study

Study the Location of the Valley of Achor
Go to the following Website for a map and read about this fascinating place in Israel: http://bibleatlas.org/valley_of_achor.htm

Devotional Thoughts

THERE'S A STARK DIFFERENCE between those who refuse to worship God by turning to idols and relying on themselves and those who are completely devoted to God.

Those who seek God's pasture land, His heavenly kingdom, will be given all the blessings of life—food, drink, joy, singing, and blessings in the land by the God of truth. Those who go after idols will go hungry, thirsty, they will be put to shame, they will cry out from anguish of heart and wail in brokenness of spirit. Their legacy will be a curse and their destiny will be death. But for those who invoke the God of truth, past troubles will be forgotten.

Response

WHICH COURSE WILL I FOLLOW TODAY? Will I depend on myself or on God? Am I devoted to me or to the Lord?

These questions are especially hard-hitting when I feel discouraged. Stress is an overwhelming mountain and I don't see anyway out of it.

 **Day 18**

However, here's a promise: that if I seek God's kingdom, if I seek God with all of my heart, soul, and mind, I will sing for joy out of my heart. My past troubles will be forgotten.

And in the midst of my trouble, the Valley of Achor (that's what Achor means—trouble), I will see prosperity and abundance!

So what am I going to choose to believe? My heart that says nothing will ever get better or God's Word?

I will, with God's help, keep seeking Him day by day, hour by hour.

And one day soon I will be singing at the top of my lungs!

Encouragement/Challenge

WHAT COURSE WILL YOU FOLLOW TODAY? Will you depend on yourself or God? To whom are you devoted? You or the Lord? Determine in your heart and spirit to seek Him no matter what your heart is telling you. Hang in there for the fulfillment of the promise and realize your troubles are momentary and light. They will not last forever, no matter how you feel right now. You too will sing at the top of your lungs! It will be quite a concert someday when we all get together!

Activity

PLAY SARDINES. This is best played at night with a lot of people. If you do not have a large family, invite some friends over and have some fun!

Blessings Journey

But put a twist on this game. The person who hides in the dark is the King (or Queen). The others are to search and find that King (or Queen) and get as close to him or her as possible, until everyone is squished in that tiny place in the dark.

Talk about how important it is to seek after God, our King, especially when times are tough and it feels like someone has turned out the lights! And when we snuggle up close to Him, He brings us comfort and pretty soon we can sing for joy!

Prayer

Dear Heavenly Father, we praise You that You alone are worthy of our worship! Thank You that our troubles are momentary and when we seek You with all our hearts, we will find joy again. Help us to choose day by day to follow You. *In Jesus' Name, Amen.*

> "The LORD bless you,
> and keep you; The LORD make His
> face shine on you, And be gracious to
> you; The LORD lift up His
> countenance on you,
> And give you peace."
>
> —Numbers 6:25–26, *New American Standard Bible*

Prayer

Dear Lord, we praise You that You are worth living for and dying for! Thank You for dying for us! Help us to bless our enemies even in the face of persecution. *In Jesus' Name, Amen.*

Worship

"It is Well with my Soul"
Vineyard Music

Even when we're persecuted, we can say it is well with our souls!

Scripture

Romans 12:9–21

Romans 12:14, NASB

"Bless those who persecute you; bless and do not curse."

Day 19

What Does God Say About Blessings?

What Is My Response?

For Further Study

Read About a Modern-Day Martyr, Jim Elliot
You can Google him or search at Christianity.com. They have a history on him.

You can also watch the movie, *The End of the Spear.* This movie is told from the perspective of Steve Saint, the son of the pilot Nate Saint who was also killed that day in 1956. But it is a graphic movie so use your discretion in watching it with little ones.

Devotional Thoughts

I HAVE BEEN GIVEN BLESSINGS, now I have a choice—bless or curse those who persecute me. Of course, in the days of Paul it was a life or death issue. What do I face?

The persecution of former neighbors because we chose to do the right thing for our family.

I can respond evil for evil (how tempting it is to get sweet revenge!) or bless them in prayer and in deeds. When they are hungry, when they are thirsty... So I have to see a need and fill it. And instead of arguing with them...

We chose to move from an old neighborhood to a newer one in Colorado Springs because it was best for our family, and because of our decision, we came to realize that homeschooling was our best option for education.

Especially because we came to discover our son and my husband are probably high-functioning Autistics!

We remodeled our old house (an 1898 Victorian) and turned it into a vacation rental. While our guests loved it, our neighbors were completely against it. But in-

 # Day 19

stead of bringing up their honest concerns in a mature manner, they screamed at us, swore at us, called city code on us, and plotted to ruin our business.

Instead of cursing them back, we had a plan on how to deal with any confrontations. It never came up, but having the plan (see below) helped. We gave them what they wanted: we gave up the business and put the house up for sale. We discovered that running a vacation rental was not for us.

But along the way, having two mortgages and not enough income was extremely burdensome. It would be very easy to curse them. But I have spent time instead praying blessings over them.

Interestingly enough, the housing in that area plummeted so much that after a failed short sale, our house foreclosed in September of 2010.

Our neighbors' house values plummeted even more than it already has.

While we did not plot for this kind of revenge, God has given them their just rewards. We made room for His wrath!

And I thank God that He delivered us from that neighborhood! If we had still been living there, we would have nothing! And we would be trapped because sooner or later the true natures of our neighbors would have come out. That neighborhood and house was not a good place to raise our son!

Somehow God will deliver us from the financial fallout. I don't see it right now, but even so, I must live a life of blessing, even for those who persecute me.

Response

RESPOND WITH BLESSINGS, NOT CURSES. So, when encountering those who persecute me, be pleasant as possible.

If confronted, have a plan: Ask them:

1. What is it that you want me to do?

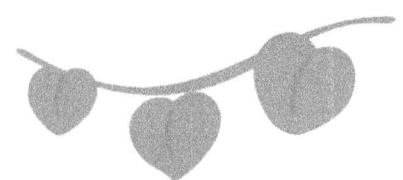

2. Don't talk to me like that. I don't like it.
3. I'd be glad to talk to you when you are calm.
    Then walk away.

It's good for me to read this plan again. I wrote it several years ago, inspired by the lessons learned in the *Love and Logic* program.

I wish I had had this plan many years ago when I had an unpleasant confrontation with someone in the old neighborhood. My dogs had escaped and my son and I were on our way to get them. A neighbor was walking her dogs and started yelling at me, I mean **really** yelling at me. I yelled back, but I yelled back **blessings!** It was such a weird confrontation. If I had had that plan, I wonder how it might have changed that whole scene? This confrontation plan can also help with confrontations between family members. Use it the next time a heated argument comes up!

Encouragement/ Challenge

WHAT IS *YOUR* PLAN FOR FACING PERSECUTION? Is it to curse or bless? Are you looking for revenge or are you trusting in God, leaving room for His wrath? Come up with a plan. Our persecution in the United States is not that threatening yet, but as time goes by, the consequences of living for God may become worse and worse. For instance, a pastor on Facebook wrote that he has a plan in case he is sent to jail for sticking up for his faith. In some countries, if you homeschool your children, you can be sent to jail or have the kids taken away from you. This kind of persecution

Day 19

could be just around the corner. Are you ready? And in the meantime, what are we doing to protect our freedoms? The threat of terrorism is getting ever closer, as witnessed by the horrific shootings in Paris recently, and radical Islamic fascists are beheading Christians in the Middle East. So be vigilant in prayer and get involved!

Activity

Have a family movie night! Watch *The End of the Spear* or another movie about Christian martyrs. The old classic *The Robe* comes to mind. Make popcorn, watch the movie, and then talk about the persecution the early Christians faced and contrast it with the persecution we face today. Discuss how persecution happens in other countries and how our own country is more and more becoming a place where Christians are put down for their faith. Talk about how you and your family can reach out in a post-modern, post-Christian world and show the love of Christ to others who don't know Him, even if that means some type of persecution.

Prayer

Our Father, we thank You for loving us so much that You gave Your only Son to die in our place. Help us to love You faithfully and keep blessing others, even when we are made fun of for following You, or even worse. Help us in these times when more and more persecution is becoming more and more of a reality, and be with those in other countries who put their lives at risk to share Your gospel. *In Jesus' Name, Amen.*

Blessings Journey

"The LORD bless you,
and keep you;
The LORD make His face
shine on you,
And be gracious to you;
The LORD lift up His
countenance on you,
And give you peace."

—Numbers 6:25–26, *New American Standard Bible*

Blessings Journey Day 20

Prayer

Our Lord and Savior, thank You for loving us so much that You died for us. Help us to bring our shortcomings before You to the cross. Please forgive us for missing the mark and not loving You with our whole hearts. Thanks again for Your overwhelming grace and mercy and glory. *In Jesus' Name, Amen.*

Worship

"Here I am to Worship"
Michael W. Smith

Scripture

Leviticus 9

Leviticus 9:23–24, *NASB*

Moses and Aaron went into the tent of meeting. When they came out and blessed the people, the glory of the Lord appeared to all the people. Then fire came out from before the Lord and consumed the burnt offering and the portions of fat on the altar; and when all the people saw it, they shouted and fell on their faces.

 Day 20

What Does God Say About Blessings?

_____
_____
_____
_____
_____
_____
_____
_____
_____

What Is My Response?

_____
_____
_____
_____
_____
_____
_____
_____

For Further Study

What Does the Gospel Really Mean?

Whether you have been walking with the Lord for 20 years, a brand-new Christian, or a seeker, it's important to understand or review the true meaning of the gospel. You may also find this explanation a simple way to share with a child.

The gospel means good news. Before there can be good news, there has to be bad news. The bad news is that we all have sinned, we all have missed the mark, and fallen short of the glory of God (Romans 3:23) and that the wages or payday of this sin is death, of being eternally separated from God. It's like standing at the edge of the Grand Canyon. No effort on our own will bring us to the other side! This is because God is holy and He can have nothing to do with sin.

The good news is that God loved you so much that He sent His son to die for you so you might live with Him forever (John 3:16). He is offering you a free gift, eternal salvation, which means you will have a forever personal relationship with Jesus.

What does He want you to do? Accept the gift! Believe in faith that Jesus is the Son of God, died on the cross, and was raised from the dead, that He is your personal Lord and Savior. Receive Him as Lord and Savior, ask Him to live in your heart, to be in every part of you, the center of every aspect of your life (John 1:12). To trust Him alone for your salvation. Then celebrate that you have eternal life (1 John 5:12–13)!

For more information on the gospel, go to the following Website that explains it very thoroughly:

http://www.navigators.org/Tools/Evangelism%20Resources/Tools/The%20Bridge%20to%20Life

Day 20

Devotional Thoughts

Going from stress to blessings, going from sin to glory, darkness to light—
It's not instant and it costs. God appearing in His shining glory does not come cheaply. Because there's a big problem to overcome—sin and the darkness that the darkness of sin brings to my soul.

Aaron and his sons shed blood of a calf and sprinkled it on the altar. After they were done, they came out and blessed the people, and the glory of God appeared to all the people and God consumed the offering with fire as God's glory blazed out and all the people witnessed it and cheered loudly and bowed in reverence.

But what does this story mean for today, when we don't use these rituals and God does not appear en masse, or at all as it seems, for that matter...?

God wants to shine in my heart, He wants to show me His glory but He cannot exist near evil, near sin, near darkness, so He sent His Son to die in my place. He was the sacrificial atonement, it cost Him His life and a lot of pain. He left the comfort and safety of heaven and came down to a messy world.

And He paid a huge price for that, a huge price for me. So that He could shine in my heart and appear before me in glory and I would cheer loudly in victory and bow before Him in reverence.

Response

Come before the cross. Live the gospel. Bring my stress to Him as a living sacrifice. Bow before Him in reverence. Trust in His glory for my victory and cheer Him.

Encouragement/Challenge

ARE YOU LIVING THE GOSPEL EVERY DAY? Do you understand what the gospel means? Bring your stress to Him as a living sacrifice (Romans 12:1) and determine to give away your faith to someone. Sharing the gospel with someone, perhaps a child or a person who does not have a personal relationship with Jesus, will help you understand the gospel better!

Activity

BUILD A TABERNACLE 3D PUZZLE together and discuss the parts of the Tabernacle and why God said to make them that way. There are many different kinds available. Christianbook.com is one place you can purchase such a puzzle.

Prayer

OUR LOVING LORD, we praise You that You are glorious, more glorious than we could ever imagine. We bow down before You and give You our lives. Shine in our hearts so we can be a display for Your glory. *In Jesus' Name, Amen.*

Day 20

> "The LORD bless you,
> and keep you;
> The LORD make His face
> shine on you,
> And be gracious to you;
> The LORD lift up His
> countenance on you,
> And give you peace."
> —Numbers 6:25–26, *New American Standard Bible*

Blessings Journey Day 21

Prayer

Everlasting Lord, thank You for blessing us through Abraham so long ago. You had a plan and proved faithful to Your promises. Help us to live by faith in You and not man-made laws. *In Jesus' Name, Amen.*

Worship

"God Will Make a Way"

Scripture

Galatians 3

Galatians 3:6–9, *NASB*

Even so Abraham believed God, and it was reckoned to him as righteousness. Therefore, be sure that it is those who are of faith who are sons of Abraham. The Scripture, foreseeing that God would justify the Gentiles by faith, preached the gospel beforehand to Abraham, saying, "All the nations will be blessed in you." So then those who are of faith are blessed with Abraham, the believer.

 Day 21

What Does God Say About Blessings?

What Is My Response?

For Further Study

Read Luke 6:1–11

How does Jesus respond to the Pharisees who criticized Him for supposedly breaking the Sabbath? How does this passage illustrate the difference between living a life of grace as opposed to living a life of law?

Devotional Thoughts

EVEN SO, ABRAHAM BELIEVED GOD.

And I am his descendent by faith.

I am a daughter of Abraham. The Scripture foresaw that I would be justified by faith and proclaimed to Abraham that all nations would be blessed by Him.

So I who am in faith in Christ am blessed through Abraham, who believed God.

Living by faith is the key. Living in the Spirit, as opposed to living by the law. The law is a curse. To live by the law is a curse.

I did not receive the Spirit through my own works, but because I asked Jesus into my heart and believed that He died for my sins and rose again.

Christ redeemed me from the curse of the law. He became a curse for me.

So that in Him the blessing of Abraham might come to me. And to others through me.

That I might receive the promise of the Spirit through faith.

And since I am baptized in Christ, I am clothed with Christ. It means I have re-

 **Day 21**

sponsibility along with great freedom. It means that through Christ I can be unified with fellow believers, no matter how different they are from me. We are Abraham's seed, heirs according to the promise. But it doesn't end there. The promise given to me is so that I can share that promise with others.

Response

EVEN SO, BELIEVE. Believe in God even when all seems out of control and impossible. Realize and live the fact that I am an heir, a child of God. Do not live by the law, but by grace, the power of the Holy Spirit.

Encouragement/ Challenge

DO YOU BELIEVE EVEN WHEN LIFE'S CIRCUMSTANCES SEEM IMPOSSIBLE? Do you really believe that God will come through with His promises? Abraham believed that God would fulfill His promise, that Abraham would be the father of many nations, even though it seemed impossible at the time. Abraham, an old man, had no heir. Yet Abraham believed.

What are you living by? Are you living in faith or are you living by law? Examine your way of life—have you let man-made laws rule your life or are you living by the power of the Holy Spirit?

Activity

There are a lot of activities on the following Website for children of all ages that will teach your children about Abraham. Includes crafts, printables, coloring pages, and stories.
http://www.dltk-bible.com/genesis/chapter15-index.htm

Prayer

Sovereign Lord, we praise You that You are the God of impossibilities. No matter what our circumstances, we can believe You. Help us to have wisdom in our daily lives to live by faith, not the law. *In Jesus' Name, Amen.*

> "The LORD bless you,
> and keep you;
> The LORD make His face
> shine on you,
> And be gracious to you;
> The LORD lift up His
> countenance on you,
> And give you peace."
>
> —Numbers 6:25–26, *New American Standard Bible*

Prayer

Loving Father, we praise You that You alone can satisfy the deepest parts of our hearts. Heal us from our waywardness, from turning away from You. *In Jesus' Name, Amen.*

Worship

"All I Need is You"
Hillsong United

Scripture

Hosea 14

Blessings Journey

Hosea 14:4–8, *NASB*

"I will heal their waywardness.
I will love them lavishly. My anger is played out.
I will make a fresh start with Israel.
He'll burst into bloom like a crocus in the spring.
He'll put down deep oak tree roots,
he'll become a forest of oaks!
He'll become splendid-like a giant sequoia,
his fragrance like a grove of cedars!
Those who live near him will be blessed by him,
be blessed and prosper like golden grain.
Everyone will be talking about them,
spreading their fame as the vintage children of God.
Ephraim is finished with gods that are no-gods.
From now on I'm the one who answers and satisfies him.
I am like a luxuriant fruit tree.
Everything you need is to be found in me."

Day 22

What Does God Say About Blessings?

_____
_____
_____
_____
_____
_____
_____
_____
_____

What Is My Response?

_____
_____
_____
_____
_____
_____
_____
_____
_____

For Further Study

Hosea—A Fascinating and Beautiful Book

It's about how God loves us, even when we are unfaithful. Read this book first for yourself and then decide if you are ready to read it together as a family, as the author of this book marries a prostitute and discovers God's love in new ways through the heart-wrenching pain of his wife's unfaithfulness.

Devotional Thoughts

THIS PASSAGE IN HOSEA SPEAKS ABOUT ISRAEL'S FUTURE BLESSINGS. Here below I have rewritten this powerful passage and personalized it, putting my name in it and my particular stumbling blocks.

Return to the Lord your God for I have stumbled because of my iniquity. Take words with me and return to the Lord. Say to Him, take away all iniquity and receive me graciously that I may present the fruit of my lips.

Food, the government, get rich-quick schemes, a job, hard work, a title, being thin, being attractive...

Will not **save me.** *I will not say again my god, the work of my hands for in you I who have been abandoned find mercy.*

He will heal my apostasy, He will love me freely, His anger has turned from me. God will be like the dew to me, I will blossom like the lily, and I will take root... My shoots will sprout.

And my beauty will be like the olive tree and my fragrance like the cedars of Lebanon.

Day 22

Those who live in my shadow will again raise grain and they will blossom like the vine. My renown will be like the wine of Lebanon.

"O Dana, what more have I to do with idols?

It is I who answer and look after you. I am like a luxuriant cypress; from Me comes your fruit.

If you are wise, understand these things. If you are discerning, know them. For My ways are right and you, as a redeemed child of God, will walk in them."

Response

IN THIS TIME OF STRESS AND UNCERTAINTY, cling to Him even more. He will be like the dew to me. Trust that God will look after me. Do what He has called me to do, but again, leave the results to Him!

Encouragement/Challenge

INSERT YOUR NAME AND YOUR PARTICULAR stumbling blocks in this passage that I have written above. Go to Him in serious prayer. If it is helpful, print your personalized verse and post it where you can read it often. Cling to Him alone and trust that He will look after you, and make you blossom!

Blessings Journey

Activity

Go on a nature walk early in the morning. Find where dew has settled on plants and flowers. Take photographs of it, sketch it, make paintings. Find the beauty of dew gathered on a spider web. Relate the dew you saw in nature to this passage.

Prayer

Gracious Lord, we love You and adore You. Thank You for Your beauty and Your grace. Help us to live Your blessing and be a blessing to all around us. *In Jesus' Name, Amen.*

"The LORD bless you,
and keep you;
The LORD make His face
shine on you,
And be gracious to you;
The LORD lift up His
countenance on you,
And give you peace."
—Numbers 6:25–26, *New American Standard Bible*

Blessings Journey Day 23

Prayer

Our Heavenly Father, thank You for giving us Your son. Thank you for dying for us so we could live in You. Help us to rejoice in our sufferings and to use them as opportunities to praise You. *In Jesus' Name, Amen.*

Worship

"There is a Redeemer"
Keith Green

Scripture

1 Peter 4

1 Peter 4:14, *NASB*

If you are reviled for the name of Christ, you are blessed, because the Spirit of glory and of God rests on you.

 Day 23

What Does God Say About Blessings?

_____
_____
_____
_____
_____
_____
_____
_____
_____

What Is My Response?

_____
_____
_____
_____
_____
_____
_____
_____

For Further Study

Read Corrie ten Boom's Book, *The Hiding Place*
Talk about how Corrie and her sister Betsy determined to be thankful and rejoice despite the most horrid of circumstances.

Devotional Thoughts

I AM BLESSED WHEN I AM REVILED (HATED) FOR THE NAME OF CHRIST. I am blessed when I am hated because the Spirit of glory and of God rests upon me. It is an honor, not a shame, to suffer as a Christian. In that name, in the name of Christ, I can glorify God.

As I read this passage again for this book, I don't recall being outright hated because I am a follower of Christ. But I have made decisions in my life because I've believed I was following God that have not been too popular. In fact, I have lost even Christian friends because I was obeying Jesus. It's a very lonely place to be in. I also remember arguing with a New Age believer when I was in college whether or not the nearby tree was god. She wasn't too happy that I didn't think so!

But in 2008, my husband and I took a huge step of faith, believing that He wanted us to take this step after much soul-searching and praying, *"Where do you want us, God?"* And then a couple of years later, it seemed as if life was falling apart because of this decision and I didn't see a solution.

This involved a failed rental investment property we used to live in that went into

Day 23

foreclosure after a pending short sale fell through.

I was discouraged about the stress that just wouldn't go away because of this decision and I wondered, *"Where is God in the midst of this? Didn't I get into this situation because I was following You?"* Some might think that we made a mistake or was foolish, but we believed we were following the trail God had for us. Besides, looking back and Monday-morning quarterbacking is not constructive and "woulda coulda shoulda" thinking only results in analysis to paralysis.

There were no easy answers for our situation. I was overwhelmed with the needs our family faces and years later we still have overwhelming needs. But according to this passage, I need to be clear minded and self-controlled. Because the end is near.

Now, on the face of it that sounds really scary. But only God knows the day or hour He will return. Only God knows the day or hour I will go to meet Him. The point of that statement to me is to live as if each day is my last. Loving deeply, being hospitable, not letting emotions twist my heart into fear, and most of all, using the gifts God has given me, faithfully administering God's grace in its various forms.

And right now, I am using the gifts God has given me by writing this devotional and sharing it through this book. If I suffer along the way, I need to rejoice. So that *in all things,* God may be praised through Jesus Christ!

Because really, I couldn't hold on to the old house anyway. When Jesus returns, it's not going to matter a whole lot. It's God's house, as well as the house we live in now.

But when I realize that God delivered us from that place we were living in, I am amazed and thankful! I can truly rejoice, because if we had stayed in that house we would have been trapped! Obviously, God knew the market would plummet so He got us out beforehand! He proved Himself sovereign yet again! Why am I even surprised?

Since that time, I have personally witnessed how God has sustained us. He

will keep on sustaining us. When we lost the old house to foreclosure, I could not see it. I did know that everyday I needed to remember to be thankful and rejoice despite my circumstances, even because of my circumstances, because then the Spirit of glory and of God will rest upon me. I still need to remember that going forward, even when our situation is improving and there is "light at the end of the tunnel."

Response

ENTRUST MY SOUL TO A FAITHFUL CREATOR in doing what is right. Do what's right. Let the chips fall where they may. Use my gifts to the best of my ability and leave the results up to God (funny how that one comes up again and again!). And most of all, commit myself to my faithful Creator and continue to do good (verse 19).

Encouragement/ Challenge

HOW DO YOU SUFFER FOR BEING NAMED AFTER CHRIST? Are you willing to obey Jesus no matter what, even if you are insulted? This is really hard for people pleasers, and I say this from experience because I am one!

Another question for homeschoolers and ministry leaders: have you insulated yourself so much that you are in a holy huddle? We are supposed to be salt and light to a dying world. But how can that light and salt be noticed if we are hiding in our

Day 23

"upper rooms?" We are commanded to go into all the world and make disciples, and that means we may be reviled for our faith. How can you get out of your comfort zone and become missionaries in your own backyard?

Also as homeschoolers, we may be subject to pressure by social services, parents, neighbors... If Jesus truly called you to homeschool, keep your eyes focused on Him and rejoice! God will be praised through Jesus Christ!

Activity

VOLUNTEER AS A FAMILY in a rescue mission, Habitat for Humanity, Care and Share, invite a foreign exchange student into your home for a year, invite your neighbors over for an ice cream social... These are just some ideas to get you involved in community, loving deeply, and being hospitable.

Prayer

OUR REDEEMER, we praise You that no matter what our circumstances, You are under control. Help us to believe that and live that day by day, using to Your glory the gifts You have given us. *In Jesus' Name, Amen.*

Blessings Journey

"The LORD bless you,
and keep you;
The LORD make His face
shine on you,
And be gracious to you;
The LORD lift up His
countenance on you,
And give you peace."

—Numbers 6:25–26, *New American Standard Bible*

Prayer

Our faithful Lord, we thank You for Your promises, that they are "yes" in Christ. We count on You with every fiber of our being. Help us to realize this and daily practice utter dependence on You. *In Jesus' Name, Amen.*

Worship

"You are My Strength"
Hillsong

Scripture

Haggai 2

Blessings Journey

Haggai 2:19b, *NASB*

"Yet from this day on I will bless you."

 Day 24

What Does God Say About Blessings?

_____
_____
_____
_____
_____
_____
_____
_____
_____

What Is My Response?

_____
_____
_____
_____
_____
_____
_____
_____
_____

For Further Study

Study the Role of Work in the Bible

Why is work important? Who are we to work for? What happens if we choose not to work even though we can?

Devotional Thoughts

HE SAYS TO BE STRONG AND WORK, for He is with me. He fills a temple, a God-given project, with glory and provides for its building. Perhaps destruction has happened in the past, but the seed is still there, waiting. He is the one who causes it to bear fruit through His blessings.

This chapter of Haggai, since my original devotional writing, seems even more applicable today. We work and work and yet we are sometimes confronted with scarcity, a trickle-down effect of corruption. At times, it has felt like all we have endeavored to undertake was filled with blight.

Specifically, the old house we poured our money and hard work into, and now we got nothing back for it because of this economy. In fact, we bought it for $178,000. We put at least $50,000 into it if not more, and the house, after it was foreclosed, sold for $175,000! Talk about an exercise in futility!

Yet this is the old house. Believe me, I don't miss it. We let go of that house because we eagerly anticipate what God is going to do in our new house—not just where we live but in and through our family, to be a fruitful vine, blessed and chosen

Day 24

of the Lord. His glory will shine through us because we have turned to Him and we are striving each day to obey Him, to do what He's called us to do, to keep fear at bay, and to most of all have trust that He is with us and peace and blessings will be a result of this great struggle we have been experiencing. And through this struggle, we are learning day by day to trust Him just a little bit more. Sometimes it has proven true that our hearts were more at ease, believing God would come through, even though our circumstances had not changed one bit!

Response

SEE MY RESPONSE in these two ways:

1) My body is His temple. I have destroyed it, but it belongs to Him. My part is to be strong and to work. He will be with me. He will rebuild it even better than it was!

2) School? Work? Whatever task I am faced with, I am to be strong and to work and not to fear. He is with me. He will bless the seeds I have planted that have been lying dormant!

Somehow, someway, this crazy scenario we find ourselves in will work out and we will discover joy, abundance, blessings, and peace. I need to keep turning to Jesus, having confidence in Him, while being faithful with the callings He has given me. *Since originally writing this journal entry years ago, I am seeing these words of faith come true. We are experiencing abundance like never before! And more importantly, our hearts are completely transformed.*

Blessings Journey

Encouragement/Challenge

What "buildings" have been destroyed in your life? How has destruction, defilement, and corruption corroded your life, resulting in scarcity, fear, and uncertainty?

Turn to God. He "owns" the buildings anyway, whether they are your house, your job, your 401k. The silver and gold is His. Work for Him and Him alone, let go of your fear, and look eagerly for God's abundance, peace, and blessings.

Activity

Get an ant colony or go out and study an ant hill. Learn about the role of each kind of ant and how they all work together to live in their colony. Go to the library and discover more about ants. Discuss how ants are an example to us of hard work, cooperation, and ultimately blessing.

Prayer

Faithful God, thank You for Your provision and for caring for us. Thank You that in nature You reveal to us Your beautiful character. Help us to turn to You always, trusting You for building peace, glory, and blessings into our lives. *In Jesus' Name, Amen.*

 Day 24

"The LORD bless you,
and keep you;
The LORD make His face
shine on you,
And be gracious to you;
The LORD lift up His
countenance on you,
And give you peace."

—Numbers 6:25–26, *New American Standard Bible*

Blessings Journey Day 25

Prayer

Merciful God, we magnify Your name! Thank You that You bring us incredible joy and that You can do the impossible. Help us to be Your willing servants believing that You accomplish what You have promised us. *In Jesus' Name, Amen.*

Worship

"Holy is His Name"
John Michael Talbot

Scripture

Luke 1

Luke 1:45, NASB

"And blessed is she who believed that there would be a fulfillment of what had been spoken to her by the Lord."

 # Day 25

What Does God Say About Blessings?

What Is My Response?

For Further Study

Study the Life of Johann Sebastian Bach, a Composer from the Baroque Period

Listen to the *Magnificat*. Read a biography from *Christianity Today*. Learn about Baroque music. Discover everything you want to know about Bach. Here is a Website that will get you started: http://www.jsbach.org

Devotional Thoughts

THIS CHAPTER IS PACKED! PACKED WITH BLESSINGS! There is nothing that is impossible with God—not conceiving a child for an old couple, well along in their years, not conceiving a child for a virgin, not filling an unborn child with the Holy Spirit!

The question is, how do I respond when the Lord promises the impossible? Do I ask for a sign out of a cynical heart, like Zechariah, or do I ask sincere questions and in utter humility declare, *"I am the Lord's servant, may it be to me as you have said."*?

One course of action brings confusion, as in Zechariah being silenced, and yes, God blessed tremendously despite his doubts. He still blesses when we are filled with unbelief, but perhaps slowly and at a cost.

But the other response, the response of Mary, brings blessings immediately! Blessed is she who has believed that what the Lord has said to her will be accomplished!

Day 25

Response

BELIEVE GOD'S PROMISES, that He will accomplish what He has said to me. Review the promises and post everywhere. Sing about them, make songs out of them, declare them...

Encouragement/Challenge

WHAT ARE YOU BELIEVING GOD FOR? Are you looking for a sign to bolster your faith or are you willing to believe that God can accomplish His promises for you? When reading the Bible, underline passages that stand out to you, that the Holy Spirit impresses on you as a personal promise. Date it. Post it. Memorize it. Live it!

Activity

MAKE HOMEMADE MUSICAL INSTRUMENTS! Use items you have around the home like coffee cans, cereal boxes, tissue boxes, rubber bands, paper cups, rice... your imagination is your only limit! If you want more advanced ideas, check out a book in your local library. Many craft ideas abound in making homemade musical instruments. When you finish making your instruments, be sure to have a family "concert!"

Prayer

EXALTED LORD, we praise You and adore You for Your Name is holy. You are the God of impossibilities. Thank You for Your promises. Help us to believe that You will accomplish those promises, even when circumstances seem impossible. *In Jesus' Name, Amen.*

"The LORD bless you,
and keep you;
The LORD make His face
shine on you,
And be gracious to you;
The LORD lift up His
countenance on you,
And give you peace."
—Numbers 6:25–26, *New American Standard Bible*

Blessings Journey Day 26

Prayer

Heavenly Father, thank You by wisdom You created the whole universe! You are exalted above all things! Help us to desire You above all else in our lives. *In Jesus' Name, Amen.*

Worship

"More Precious Than Silver"

Scripture

Proverbs 3:13–20

Proverbs 3:13, *NASB*

*How blessed is the man who finds wisdom
And the man who gains understanding.*

 Day 26

What Does God Say About Blessings?

What Is My Response?

For Further Study

Study the Difference between Wisdom, Knowledge, and Understanding
Search "Wisdom" in Bible Gateway. Read commentaries on Wisdom by Matthew Henry.

Devotional Thoughts

THE KEY TO BLESSING IS FINDING WISDOM AND GAINING UNDERSTANDING. It is more profitable to invest in this pursuit than 401(k)s, real estate, or business. Wisdom's rewards are long life, riches, and honor. The fruits of such a pursuit is pleasant and results in peace, life, and happiness. God founded this world on wisdom and established the heavens with His understanding. By His knowledge the deeps were broken up and the skies drip with dew.

Response

SOMETIMES THE PRICE OF THIS KIND of wisdom and understanding is painful trial and error. This is how I paid for the knowledge that my son and husband probably both have high-functioning Autism. Now that I have this knowledge, it's time to pursue wisdom, understanding, and more knowledge on how to deal with this Autism, especially for my son. I have spent years doing just that, and along the way, I have been able to help others.

 # Day 26

    I will never regret pursuing this knowledge and we will all profit from it. There will be many rewards—blessings such as peace, life, riches, and honor. And finding it and discovering it will be pleasant!

    And in terms of discovering this new world to me of Autism, it has been a huge blessing and relief. Studying about Asperger Syndrome has helped me in my marriage. It's given me more patience which has directly led to more peace! Understanding how my son's brain works has helped me make better decisions regarding his education, which has definitely led to less stress and more life!

    I have a long ways to go on this journey, but just knowing what we struggle with has helped tremendously. We are more open, more real, more transparent, and we are beginning to come out of the shadows to cultivate a supportive community based on give and take relationships.

    These days I am pursuing more understanding about Autism, especially Sensory Processing Disorder. Just implementing one idea from a book I bought on the subject brought so much blessing to my son and myself! It's time to pursue this wisdom, understanding, and knowledge from books, doctors, occupational therapists, and especially other moms who have gone through what I am going through now. *In fact, as I prepare for this book to be published, I am editing this original devotional writing while my son undergoes brain therapy. That is where all this research led me to!*

    Doing so is well worth it and will be treasure in itself, resulting in blessings beyond imagining!

Encouragement/Challenge

What knowledge, wisdom, and understanding do you need to gain? Is it a matter of digging deeper into the Word? Then do so! Do you need to ask for help? Don't hesitate, it will be well worth it! Whatever area you need to grow in, spend time diligently seeking the answers to your questions. The rewards will be blessings beyond belief!

Activity

Visit a precious gem museum, mining museum, or money mint museum. If possible, go to an interactive museum where your children can pan for gold or something similar. Let your children discover about precious gems and minerals and how money is made. Discuss how this relates to the Proverbs 3 passage. God and His wisdom is so much more precious than jewels, silver, and gold!

Prayer

Lord, You are more precious than silver and costly than gold. Show us where we lack in wisdom, knowledge and understanding, and help us to pursue You, whatever it costs! *In Jesus' Name, Amen.*

 # Day 26

> "The LORD bless you,
> and keep you;
> The LORD make His face
> shine on you,
> And be gracious to you;
> The LORD lift up His
> countenance on you,
> And give you peace."
> —Numbers 6:25–26, *New American Standard Bible*

Prayer

Amazing Lord, thank You that You love little children. We come to you with simplicity of faith and ask You to put Your hands on us and bless us. *In Jesus' Name, Amen.*

Worship

"My Heart, Your Home"
Hillsong Kids

Scripture

Mark 10

Mark 10:16, *NASB*

And He took them in His arms and began blessing them, laying His hands on them.

 Day 27

What Does God Say About Blessings?

_____
_____
_____
_____
_____
_____
_____
_____
_____

What Is My Response?

_____
_____
_____
_____
_____
_____
_____
_____
_____

For Further Study

What is the Kingdom of Heaven?

I stumbled upon this detailed Bible study from Pentecostal Bible Studies. I didn't get to read all of it, but it is packed with Scripture and commentary.

Go to this Website to find out more:
http://www.jimfeeney.org/kingdomofGodheaven.html

Devotional Thoughts

He put His hands on the children and blessed them...

Children have a special place in the heart of Jesus. So much so that He says: 1) Do not hinder them from coming to Him; and 2) those who do not receive the kingdom of God like a little child will never enter it.

How does a child receive the kingdom of heaven?

Children aren't bound to our fake sense of reality. They see beyond. Why is it that little children sometimes see angels while fussy grownups cannot, like one of my nieces who as a young child saw "blue floating things?"

I can remember when, as a little child, I asked Jesus into my heart. When I looked deep down inside, I could sense that He was there. After that day, He was my best friend. I sang songs to Him made up from my heart and I talked to Him, especially at bedtime until I would fall asleep.

To my son, Jesus is a huge part of life and heaven is real. Nurturing whole-hearted devotion to Christ is the primary focus of my homeschooling/child rearing.

Day 27

Response

For me, come to Jesus like a child. Sing to Him, talk to Him, have faith and trust in Him as a little child trusts her parents. Give Him all the complicated nonsense of being a grown up and rest in His arms, believing that He will bless me.

Grow in my relationship with the Heavenly Father, learning to trust Him day by day.

Encouragement/Challenge

How are you hindering your children from coming to Jesus? If so, how can you nurture a relationship with Jesus in your family? Has hard-hardedness crept into your life, keeping you from trusting Jesus like a little child? Do a little "house cleaning" and ask Jesus to take over your whole heart. Spend some time in His presence, enjoying Him as your Abba Father, or Daddy.

One new activity we like to do as a couple and as a family—my husband will randomly pick a Scripture, I will read it aloud, and then we pray. This brings us to the feet of Jesus as a family and is a way to let the little children come to Him. It is an extreme blessing to all of us.

Activity

As a family, research a charitable organization like Compassion International. Sponsor a child in a Third World country and have your children correspond with them. Discuss how sponsoring a child is letting them come to Jesus. Or do Operation Christmas Child and have your children pick out the gifts, with your guidance of course.

Prayer

Abba Father, we love You and adore You. We want to climb into Your lap like little children and soak up Your presence. Help us to keep trusting in You as a child trusts her daddy. *In Jesus' Name, Amen.*

"The LORD bless you, and keep you;
The LORD make His face
shine on you, And be
gracious to you;
The LORD lift up His
countenance on you,
And give you peace."

—Numbers 6:25–26, *New American Standard Bible*

Blessings Journey Day 28

Prayer

Mighty God, we praise You that in Christ we are more than conquerors. Help us to love You with whole-hearted devotion. *In Jesus' Name, Amen.*

Worship

"Sing, Sing, Sing"
Chris Tomlin

Scripture

Deuteronomy 11

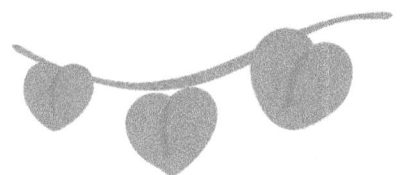

Here are some highlights of the chapter from the *New American Standard Bible:*

"You shall love the Lord your God, and always keep His charge.

You shall keep every commandment... so that you may be strong and go in and possess the land into which you are about to cross to possess it.

You shall therefore impress these words of mine on your heart and your soul, teach them to your sons, in your house and along the road, write them on the doorposts of your house and on your gates.

For if you are careful to keep all His commandments, to love the Lord your God, to walk in all His ways, and hold fast to Him, then the Lord your God will drive out all these nations and you will dispossess nations greater and mightier than you.

Verse 26: See, I am setting before you today a blessing and a curse: the blessing, if you listen to the commandments of the Lord your God, and the curse, if you do not listen."

 Day 28

What Does God Say About Blessings?

What Is My Response?

For Further Study

How Important is the Land of Israel in Our Modern times?

Do a Bible study on this topic, study the history of Israel, and discuss modern events.

One of my favorite series on this topic is by Bodie Thoene, *The Zion Chronicles*.

While I would say these books are more geared toward young adult and mature women as opposed to young children, it gives a thoughtful birds-eye view of the history of modern-day Israel and how it was founded in 1948.

Devotional Thoughts

THERE ARE ALWAYS CHOICES, ALWAYS OPTIONS. I can obey the Lord, love Him with all my heart, soul, and mind and reap rewards, victory; or I can ignore Him, and suffer the consequences—defeat.

And I am to teach this to my son, wherever I am, and write this on my doorstep.

Response

KEEP HOLDING FAST TO HIM in the midst of the uncertainty my family and I are experiencing. Remember how He has provided for me.

Learn and practice how to lay these choices out to my son. Teach him God's commands—that is to love Him with whole-hearted devotion.

Day 28

Lastly, write this on my doorstep in some tangible way, a flag or a sign out front, maybe paint some of these Scriptures on the flagstones in the garden.

Encouragement/Challenge

WHAT ARE YOUR CHOICES LEADING TO, VICTORY OR DEFEAT? Examine your relationship with the Lord. Are you seeking whole-hearted devotion of Him?

How are you teaching your children to obey God's commandments, to love Him wholeheartedly? Look for opportunities in everyday moments to teach this to your children.

Activity

MAKE A DOORPOST SIGN. Choose an excerpt from this verse, like "Love the Lord your God with all your heart, soul, and mind" or a verse like John 3:16. Have your children draw pictures on large poster board or some other material and write the verses on them. Post near your front door or gate. This would also make a fun flag project—using fabric paints draw and write the designs on material and hang up as a flag.

Blessings Journey

Prayer

Lord God, You are powerful and loving and we adore You with everything we have and are. Help us to choose Your blessings, choose Your victory, and walk with You every moment of our lives. *In Jesus' Name, Amen.*

"The LORD bless you,
and keep you;
The LORD make His face
shine on you,
And be gracious to you;
The LORD lift up His
countenance on you,
And give you peace."
—Numbers 6:25–26, *New American Standard Bible*

Prayer

Dearest Savior, in Your presence, all our doubts melt away. Help us to recognize You in every aspect of our lives. *In Jesus' Name, Amen.*

Worship

"In the Presence of Jehovah"
Damaris Carbaugh and the Brooklyn Tabernacle Choir

Scripture

John 20

John 20:29, *NASB*

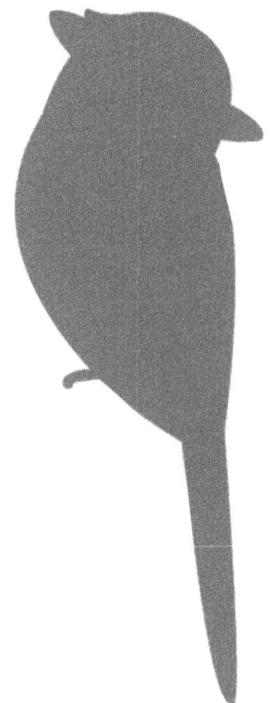

Jesus said to him, "Because you have seen Me, have you believed? Blessed are they who did not see, and yet believed."

Day 29

What Does God Say About Blessings?

_____
_____
_____
_____
_____
_____
_____
_____
_____
_____

What Is My Response?

_____
_____
_____
_____
_____
_____
_____
_____
_____

For Further Study

Fascinating Commentary

Bible Gateway has a fascinating commentary on John 20 that is packed with interesting information and illuminates this incredible chapter.

Specifically interesting to me was the section about how peace is tied to blessings. Just search under commentaries for John 20.

Devotional Thoughts

MARY AND THE DISCIPLES SAW THE LORD, both before His crucifixion and after He rose from the dead. Doubting Thomas put his fingers in Jesus' nail holes and believed.

I have only caught glimpses of the Lord, in dreams, and I love to watch re-enactments of the gospels, to see His story fleshed out visually—

But to touch Him? To hug Him as Mary did, even if briefly?

On this side of eternity, we can't sense Him through sight or touch or smell. Maybe sometimes we hear Him, but for me it's more of a still, inner voice and He speaks through the Scriptures.

Yet He says, "Blessed are those who have not seen and yet have believed."

I remember considering the claims of Christ, 10 years after I asked Him into my heart, leading up to the decision I made to follow Him as Lord—Jesus existed; this is an incontrovertible fact, no matter what people in this modern age might say. And His original followers died for Him willingly. Why would they lay down their lives for a lie?

 Day 29

Then I encountered the Holy Spirit, thick and real, in a Christian conference center. I started to seriously study the Bible, asking questions every step of the way.

After several months of this, I found with joy that I wanted to belong heart, soul, and mind to Jesus Christ and to His family. I gave my life to Him and He changed me completely.

Now flash forward nearly 30 years later. There have been many ups and downs during those years; successes, yes, but also tremendous failures.

And then incredible stress came to us, which brought the recognition all over again that I need Him utterly. Almost like I've come full circle, like when I was a child sweetly clinging to her best friend, Jesus.

And I can picture Him smiling at me now. "I am blessed," He's saying. Because I believed. I believe that He'll work through this mess even though I can't see the end result. I plod on, I am not giving up, I am waiting and hoping for Him to show up in a big way… And He is showing up in big ways.

As the saying goes—seeing is not believing, believing is seeing.

Response

KEEP BELIEVING, EVEN THOUGH I CAN'T SEE THE RESULTS OR THE END OF MY STRESS. Picture Him smiling at me as I keep seeing Him and practicing His presence no matter what.

Encouragement/Challenge

In what ways are you struggling with doubt? Are you asking to see before you can believe? If so, say this prayer that a boy's father exclaimed to Jesus, "I believe, help me in my unbelief (Mark 9:24)." God will help you believe so you can see!

Activity

Play follow the leader but choose the "it" person to be "blind." Blindfold him and have another person lead him around the house or outdoors. If you have a large family or group, you can do this in pairs.

This is a trust-building exercise. Discuss how losing one sense makes the other senses stronger. Relate it to depending on Jesus in faith rather than relying on our "sight," what we discover through the five senses.

Prayer

Lord God Jehovah, we praise You for being the Prince of Peace. Help us in our times of doubt and help us to keep believing so we can truly see. *In Jesus' Name, Amen.*

Day 29

"The LORD bless you,
and keep you;
The LORD make His face
shine on you,
And be gracious to you;
The LORD lift up His
countenance on you,
And give you peace."
—Numbers 6:25–26, *New American Standard Bible*

Prayer

Thank you, Jesus, that You are gentle and humble in nature and we can come to You anytime for true rest. Help us to lay down our busy lives and choose to sit at Your feet. *In Jesus' Name, Amen.*

Worship

"Above All"

Scripture

Genesis 2

Genesis 2:1–4, *The Message*

Heaven and Earth were finished, down to the last detail.

By the seventh day
God had finished his work.
On the seventh day
he rested from all his work.
God blessed the seventh day.
He made it a Holy Day
Because on that day he rested from his work,
all the creating God had done.

 Day 30

What Does God Say About Blessings?

_____
_____
_____
_____
_____
_____
_____
_____
_____

What Is My Response?

_____
_____
_____
_____
_____
_____
_____
_____
_____

For Further Study

Study the Sabbath in the Scriptures
What is it? Why was it made? How did Jesus view it? Who is in charge of the Sabbath? How did the Pharisees and Sadducees make man-made rules to put wearisome burdens on people? Where did Christians worshipping on Sundays come from?

Devotional Thoughts

GOD DID NOT HOLD ANYTHING BACK. He created in detail and completely finished the work. He worked hard and diligently for six days and then rested on the seventh. He called that day blessed because He rested.

Resting is not a curse. It is a blessing, a much needed respite after working diligently. Blessing comes when I work and create and give it all I've got. When I finish the work to every last detail. But when I've finished the project, it is a blessing to rest.

In our culture, we swing to two extremes—either we work and work until we're sick or even dying or we are lazy and don't finish anything or work half-heartedly. Thus the culture of incompetence we live in today.

Then there's perfectionism. There's a difference between that and excellence. Perfectionism is pride in your ego, you want to glorify yourself. Excellence is taking pride in your work because you want to glorify God.

What God blesses is a balance of hard work, creative work we can take pride in (again, not for self-glory but for God's glory), and a time of rest to revel in our accomplishments and recharge our batteries for the next creative project.

Day 30

This passage strikes me again as relevant as at the time of my original journey entry, I finished two weeks of very hard work. I scrubbed my house from top to bottom and finished painting two rooms.

Now, as I originally wrote this, I sat out on my back patio, I reveled in this little rest. Yes, writing these devotionals is a huge source of rest to me. But beyond that, I was determined to take a few days off, especially from house cleaning and painting.

I try to do this on a daily basis as well, a balance between physical work, "brain" work, and rest. It's a challenge sometimes, but I know that life is not a sprint, it's a marathon. I therefore have to pace myself!

Response

A RENEWED COMMITMENT TO WORK HARD on what God's given to me and a commitment to regularly resting. To surround myself with blessing, especially after working hard.

Encouragement/Challenge

HOW DO YOU VIEW WORK and how do you view rest? What are you modeling to your children? Does it line up with what you teach them? Evaluate this area of your life and strive for balance!

Activity

STUDY DINOSAURS FROM A CHRISTIAN WORLD VIEWPOINT. There are many wonderful resources on this subject and it is extremely fascinating!

Here are two sites to get you started:

An article from the Christian Courier:
https://www.christiancourier.com/articles/93-dinosaurs-and-the-bible

Answers In Genesis:
https://answersingenesis.org/education/study-guides/great-dinosaur-mystery-solved/lesson-1/

Prayer

FAITHFUL GOD, we extol You for the way You created this world. You are a God of wonders. Help us to view work and rest the way You view work and rest. *In Jesus' Name, Amen.*

> "The LORD bless you, and keep you;
> The LORD make His face
> shine on you, And be gracious to you;
> The LORD lift up His countenance on
> you, And give you peace."
> —Numbers 6:25–26, *New American Standard Bible*

Blessings Journey Day 31

Prayer

Blessed Lord, we thank You that we are utterly dependent on You. Help us to follow You with whole-hearted devotion. *In Jesus' Name, Amen.*

Worship

"Blessed Be Your Name"
Robin Mark

Scripture

Matthew 5:1–12

Blessed are those who are...

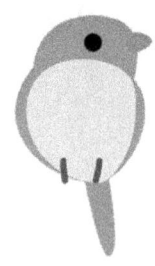

NIV (1984 Version)	The Message
poor in spirit	at the end of your rope
those who mourn	lost what is most dear to you
meek	content with just who you are
hunger and thirst for righteousness	work up a good appetite for God
merciful	when you care
pure in heart	inside world mind and heart put right
peacemakers	show people how to cooperate instead of compete
persecuted, insulted, evil said against you	commitment to God provokes persecution, put down, thrown out, spoken lies about you to discredit Jesus

 # Day 31

What Does God Say About Blessings?

What Is My Response?

For Further Study

Read Romans 12:1–2

What does it mean to offer your bodies as living sacrifices? How is this your spiritual act of worship? How can we avoid conforming to this world and instead be transformed? How can we renew our minds? Why is it important to live this verse?

Read 2 Corinthians 10:1–6

What do strongholds mean? What kind of battle do we wage? How do we get power? How can you take captive every thought to make it obedient to Christ?

Devotional Thoughts

WHAT DOES IT MEAN TO BE BLESSED?
Happy, satisfied, overflowing with love when I, out of a heart of commitment, have whole-hearted devotion to Jesus Christ, and recognize that I don't have it all together.

• Have a sorrowful heart, a grief over sin, a longing for something more, for Someone more.

• Realize I do not have the power to make it on my own nor do I need to exert power over others.

• Want God's holiness more than wanting instant gratification.

• Extend grace and truly empathize with the pain of others.

• Have a whole-hearted devotion, given over 100 percent to Jesus Christ.

Day 31

- More concerned about God's holiness and mercy to others than being right.
- Am made fun of, mocked, laughed at, scorned, hated, plotted against because of my love for Jesus.

Response

UTTER DEPENDENCE ON GOD. That's what I keep thinking as Independence Day looms ahead at the time of this writing.

I declare I am utterly dependent on God.

I don't know the end result of all this stress I'm experiencing—the overwhelming debt, the failed investment property, the care my special needs son requires...

But what I do know is I am to be transformed. I am not to be conformed to the world—the world with its fears, stresses, status symbols, materialism...

I am to be transformed—utterly dependent on God while independent from the world—so I might prove the good and acceptable and perfect will of God.

That is the keystone of the Blessed *not* Stressed lifestyle.

Taking captive every thought (stress, fear, bitterness, etc) obedient to Christ, offering our bodies as living sacrifices; this is my acceptable act of worship (Romans 12:1–2 and 2 Corinthians 10:5).

When I do that, I am truly living in blessings. It's a journey, it's a learning experience, and sometimes—many times—I fail, but when I consistently walk on this path, great blessings await me, because He can do immeasurably more than I can ask or think and I can do all things through Christ who strengthens me (Ephesians 3:20).

Encouragement/Challenge

What does it mean to you to be blessed? Read Matthew 5:1–12 and write the Beatitudes in your own words in one column. Write the result for living that way in the next column, then in a third column write your applications. Now go for it and turn your stress into blessings! Remember you can always write in this book. I've left plenty of blank space!

Activity

Play "Capture Thoughts"—Write or draw negative thoughts that set themselves up against the knowledge of God. Choose a person to be "it" and have the other children carry the signs. Now the "it" person tries to tag the children with the signs, capturing the thoughts!

Prayer

Dear Lord, we praise You for giving us the power to demolish strongholds and to hold every thought captive in obedience to You. Help us to live a life of blessing, a life of Beatitude as Your son taught. *In Jesus' Name, Amen.*

 Day 31

"The LORD bless you,
and keep you;
The LORD make His face
shine on you,
And be gracious to you;
The LORD lift up His
countenance on you,
And give you peace."
—Numbers 6:25–26, *New American Standard Bible*

What Did I Learn About Blessings?

_____
_____
_____
_____
_____
_____
_____
_____
_____
_____
_____
_____
_____
_____
_____
_____
_____

How Will I Apply It To My Life?

About the Author

Dana Susan Beasley

DANA SUSAN BEASLEY IS PRINCIPAL/PUBLISHER of *AngelArts, A Creative Arts Agency & Publishing House.* She enjoys studying the Bible and journaling, a discipline she learned starting in college after a life-transforming encounter with the campus Christian group CSU Navigators. She loves to write devotionals, Bible studies, and inspirational anthologies that point hurting people to the love and comfort of God the Father.

Dedicated to providing excellently-designed and written books, ebooks, homeschooling curriculum, cards, stationery, gifts, and art services to homeschooling families, inspirational artists, entrepreneurs, and art enthusiasts, Dana delights in sharing her gifts and talents and the talents of others with people who are passionate about spiritual, personal, educational, professional, ministerial, artistic, and relational growth.

Dana, as an entrepreneurial specialist, helps business owners and homeschooling families create sizzling brands and businesses for themselves so they can experience dazzling futures!

Blessings Journey

She is the creator of an online branding training program and entrepreneurial homeschooling curriculum, as well as audio training programs, Bible studies, devotionals, and homeschooling poetry unit studies.

Married to Travis Beasley, Dana is a homeschooling mother to her Asperger son, Sam. She helped her husband start his architectural business, Essential Pillar Architecture, and assists him with marketing and administration.

The Beasleys live in Colorado Springs, Colorado, where Dana loves to decorate their "faux" Victorian house.

The Beasleys enjoy camping, time with extended family, music, history, and their pets.

They particularly delight in their work at homeschooling lifestyle. Creativity and out-of-the box thinking keeps them inspired and productive. Combining business, homeschooling, and family time is especially rewarding to them, like when they traveled to Cheyenne, Wyoming and explored the Curt Gowdy State Park. While there, the family discussed a new novel that would combine Sam's language arts studies and history studies and Dana's business.

Or recently when Sam and Dana traveled to Albuquerque, New Mexico where they visited family, went to the Albuquerque International Balloon Fiesta, and visited a local history museum.

About the Publisher

AngelArts

ANGELARTS, A CREATIVE ARTS AGENCY & PUBLISHING HOUSE, exists to help individuals and families reach new heights in their lives and beyond through branding and marketing training and resources, homeschooling curriculum, and inspirational products and publishing.

If you like this book, you'll love Dana's products and services at **AngelArts.biz** that will help you reach new heights in your life, home, relationships, homeschooling, business, ministry, and artistry. Her products and services range from unique gifts and cards that will inspire your friends, family and associates and *you*; to books, homeschooling curriculum, and informational products that will transform your life *today;* to brand marketing and product design that will make your business stand out above the crowd!

While Dana's expertise is in graphic arts, writing, publishing, and music, she also is a homeschooling mother devoted to working at home. Her desire is that AngelArts, and her work, will be a vehicle for God's glory. Because she is always reaching for new heights

in her life and beyond and wants to inspire others to do the same!

Why the name **AngelArts?** Because excellence in art and literature is very important to Dana, and inspirational art is her passion. The company's mission, as Dana envisions it, is to be a vehicle. A vehicle for God's glory, a vehicle for artists to grow in their careers, and a vehicle for her own gifts and talents to grow and help others in publishing, graphic arts, writing, and music.

Dana chose the name AngelArts because ever since she was a little girl she has been reaching for the arts. Her mother, Ann Neal, took this photograph of her when she was a toddler, complete with tinsel halo above her head. She was always reaching for the piano, Mrs. Neal says, and wanted to learn from a young age. She finally was able to get lessons at age seven and is still playing (when time and homeschooling duties allow) on the same piano years later!

If you liked this devotional, you will love Dana's live presentations! She is available on a limited basis to speak at women's groups, networking groups, retreats, and churches. Her presentation, *3 Biblically-Based Fool-Proof Strategies that Will Transform Your Stress into Blessings,* **can also include her singing and playing original songs on piano and guitar.**

Thank you for taking the time to read this book! ***Together we can reach new heights in our lives and beyond!***

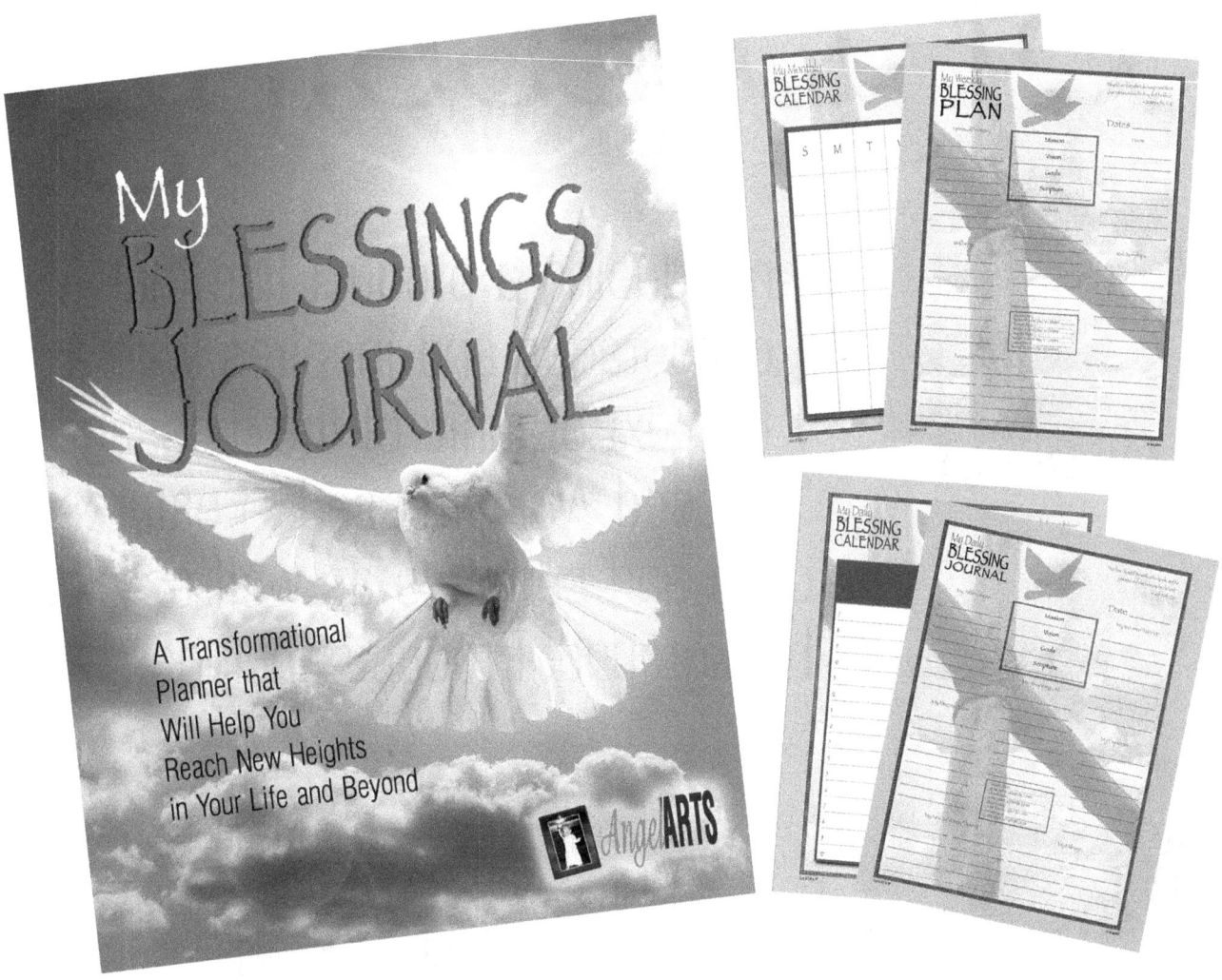

Give the Gift of Blessing!

Introducing a product line that encourages and inspires with a fun text graphic of the message "Blessed *Not* Stressed." Features dove and sun rays as well as cloud background. Products include:

- Journals
- Tshirts
- Bumper stickers
- Hoodies
- Hats
- Teddy Bears

- Magnets
- Cards
- Mugs
- Magnets
- Mousepads
- And more coming!

AngelArtsBoutique.com

www.ingramcontent.com/pod-product-compliance
Lightning Source LLC
Chambersburg PA
CBHW062127160426
43191CB00013B/2224